Activities
for a
Differentiated
Classroom

Developed by

Wendy Conklin, M.A.

Consultant

Chandra C. Prough, M.S.Ed.
National Board Certified
Newport-Mesa
Unified School District

Contributing Authors

Kelly Jones
Stephanie Kuligowski

Publishing Credits

Dona Herweck Rice, *Editor-in-Chief*; Lee Aucoin, *Creative Director*; Don Tran, *Print Production Manager*; Timothy J. Bradley, *Illustration Manager*; Chris McIntyre, M.A.Ed., *Editorial Director*; Sara Johnson, M.S.Ed., *Senior Editor*; Aubrie Nielsen, M.S., *Associate Education Editor*; Robin Erickson, *Interior Layout Designer*; Juan Chavolla, *Production Artist*; Karen Lowe, *Illustrator*; Stephanie Reid, *Photo Editor*; Corinne Burton, M.S.Ed., *Publisher*

Image Credits

p.126 (top) Anton Foltin/Shutterstock, (bottom) Gen Productions/Shutterstock; p.127 (top left) ClimberJAK/Shutterstock, (top right) Michael Woodruff/Shutterstock, (bottom left) Andrew Dunn/wikimedia, (bottom right) Ruth Black/Shutterstock

Shell Education

5301 Oceanus Drive
Huntington Beach, CA 92649-1030
http://www.shelleducation.com
ISBN 978-1-4258-0736-8
© 2011 by Shell Educational Publishing, Inc.
Reprinted 2013

The classroom teacher may reproduce copies of materials in this book for classroom use only. The reproduction of any part for an entire school or school system is strictly prohibited. No part of this publication may be transmitted, stored, or recorded in any form without written permission from the publisher.

Table of Contents

Introduction

Language Arts Lessons

Mathematics Lessons

Science Lessons

Social Studies Lessons

Appendices

Understanding Differentiation

As I conduct workshops with teachers of all ages and grade levels, I hear a familiar tune: *Differentiating curriculum is worrisome and stressful.* I believe this is due to the fact that teachers do not know how to begin differentiating. Their administrators tell them that they must differentiate, but teachers are overwhelmed with the task of doing it because there is not a clear explanation of what to do. Teachers know the theory. They know they need to do it. They just do not know *how* to do it.

The right way to differentiate depends on the unique students in a classroom. To successfully differentiate, teachers must first know their students. Knowing what academic level students are at helps us understand where to begin. When we have students who do not succeed, we find out why they are not succeeding. Then, we look for the type of support that they need to help them learn specific concepts. We make adjustments when students have trouble comprehending material. We look for new ways to present information, new manipulatives that make sense, and opportunities to provide additional support. As our struggling students grow, we can then scaffold the amount of support that we provide so that students continue to grow instead of leaning too heavily on that support. Differentiation is about meeting the needs of *all* students and providing the right amount of challenge for *all* students.

What Should I Differentiate and Why?

Many teachers have heard the terms *content*, *process*, and *product* when it comes to differentiating curriculum, but few have the time to ponder how these words apply to what they do in their classrooms. Below is a chart that briefly defines how we differentiate and why we differentiate.

Differentiating Curriculum

How	Why
Vary the Content (what is taught)	**Readiness** (students are not at the same academic level)
Vary the Process (how it is taught)	**Learning Styles** (students prefer different ways of learning)
Vary the Product (what students produce)	**Interests** (students have different passions)

Differentiation Strategies in This Book

What Differentiation Strategies Can I Use?

Each book in the *Activities for a Differentiated Classroom* series introduces a selection of differentiation strategies. Each lesson in this book uses one of the six differentiation strategies outlined below. The strategies are used across different curriculum areas and topics to provide you with multiple real-world examples.

Differentiation Strategy		Lessons in This Book
	Tiered Assignments	• Main Idea and Supporting Details—*Language Arts* • Geometric Transformations—*Mathematics* • States of Matter—*Science* • Map Skills—*Social Studies*
	Tiered Graphic Organizers	• Summarizing—*Language Arts* • Measuring and Graphing—*Mathematics* • Life Cycles—*Science* • American Indians and the Environment—*Social Studies*
	Leveled Questions	• Self-Editing—*Language Arts* • Fractions—*Math* • Erosion—*Science* • State Government—*Social Studies*
	Multiple Intelligences	• Haiku Poetry—*Language Arts* • Decimals—*Mathematics* • How Animals Adapt—*Science* • History's Heroes—*Social Studies*
	Menu of Options	• Writing Dialogue—*Language Arts* • Perimeter and Area—*Mathematics* • The Water Cycle and Weather—*Science* • Supply and Demand—*Social Studies*
	Choices Board	• Story Elements—*Language Arts* • Number Sense—*Mathematics* • The Moon—*Science* • The Age of Exploration—*Social Studies*

Tiered Assignments

One way to ensure that all students in a classroom advance—using the same skills and ideas regardless of readiness levels—is to tier lessons. Often referred to as *scaffolding*, tiered assignments offer multilevel activities based on key skills at differing levels of complexity. One example of this is leveled reading texts. All students can learn about the Civil War by reading texts that are leveled according to the different reading abilities in the classroom. You can also provide comprehension questions that are leveled. Each student comes away with essential grade-appropriate skills in addition to being sufficiently challenged. The entire class works toward one goal (learning about the Civil War), but the path to that goal depends on each student's readiness level.

So, how do you tier lessons?

- **Pick the skill, concept, or strategy that needs to be learned.** For example, a key concept would be using reading skills and strategies to understand and interpret a variety of informational texts.

- **Think of an activity that teaches this skill, concept, or strategy.** For this example, you could have students summarize the information and include a main idea in the summary.

- **Assess students.** You may already have a good idea of your students' readiness levels, but you can further assess them through classroom discussions, quizzes, tests, or journal entries. These assessments can tell you if students are above grade level, on grade level, or below grade level.

- **Take another look at the activity you developed.** How complex is it? Where would it fit on a continuum scale? Is it appropriate for above-grade-level learners, on-grade-level learners, below-grade-level learners, or English language learners?

- **Modify the activity to meet the needs of the other learners in the class.** Try to get help from the specialists in your school for English language learners, special education students, and gifted learners. For this example, summarizing with a main idea would be appropriate for on-grade-level students. Above-grade-level students should include supporting details in their summaries. The below-grade-level students will need a few examples provided for their summaries. English language learners will begin with the same examples given to below-grade-level students so that they understand what is expected of them. Then, they will summarize information verbally to you.

Remember, just because students are above grade level does not mean that they should be given more work. And, just because students are below grade level does not mean that they should be given less work. Tiered lessons are differentiated by varying the *complexity*, not necessarily the *quantity* of work required for the assignment. Likewise, all tiered activities should be interesting and engaging.

Differentiation Strategies in This Book *(cont.)*

Tiered Graphic Organizers

One way to improve the learning and performance of diverse students across grade levels in a wide range of content areas is by utilizing graphic organizers in classroom lessons. Graphic organizers are visual representations that help students gather and sort information, see patterns and relationships, clarify concepts, and organize information. Graphic organizers have a way of connecting several pieces of isolated information by taking new information and fitting it into an existing framework. Old information is retrieved in the process, and the new information is attached. By using graphic organizers in the classroom, teachers are helping students make connections and assimilate new information with what they already know.

Understanding how the brain works helps us understand why graphic organizers are valuable tools for learning. Educational brain research says that our brains seek patterns so that information can become meaningful. In her book, Karen Olsen (1995) states, "From brain research we have come to understand that the brain is a pattern-seeking device in search of meaning and that learning is the acquisition of mental programs for using what we understand." Other researchers believe that graphic organizers are one of the most powerful ways to build semantic memories (Sprenger 1999). Eric Jensen (1998) states that semantic memory is "activated by association, similarities, or contrasts." Graphic organizers assist students with such necessary connections.

The brain does this by storing information similar to how a graphic organizer shows information. It screens large amounts of information and looks for patterns that are linked together. The brain is able to extract meaning more easily from a visual format like a graphic organizer than from written words on a page. Graphic organizers not only help students manage information, they also offer information in a way that students can understand at a glance. When these connections happen, the brain transfers the information from short-term memory to long-term memory. This means that teachers who use graphic organizers help their students manage all of the information with which they are presented each day.

Because students are at different readiness levels, it makes sense to differentiate lessons with tiered graphic organizers. Some teachers worry that students will copy from other students who have additional examples on their graphic organizers. They also note that some of their students do not like to be singled out with modified work. This can be resolved by assigning groups different types of graphic organizers within one lesson. An example of this would be to give one group Venn diagrams, another group T-charts, and a third group matrices. The information can still be scaffolded as needed, but more discreetly because the organizers are different.

Differentiation Strategies in This Book (cont.)

Leveled Questions

Leveling questions means adjusting the language of a question to the different levels of student readiness. The key to leveling questions is to make the questions accessible for *all* students. Most questioning strategies can be used in whole-group discussions, but it does not make sense to use leveled questions in this way. Leveled questions should be used in small homogeneous group discussions or in written assignments for students to answer individually. The following paragraphs outline a few guidelines for leveling questions for your students.

Below-grade-level students need narrowed questions, vocabulary support, and examples. While trying to level questions for below-grade-level students, some teachers make the mistake of asking for less. For example, if the on-grade-level question asks students to find the area and perimeter of a shape, the teacher might ask the below-grade-level student to find only the perimeter. This is not a leveled question. A leveled question will still ask for the same information, but use added support to help these students answer the question.

English language learners need context added to the questions. This might be in the form of pictures or small icons directly next to key words. English language learners also benefit from simplified questions preceded by guiding statements. For example, an on-grade-level question is *What is the average of this set of data?* It could be modified for English language learners as: *Look at this set of data. What is the average?* As English language learners read the question, they know right away that the question is about the set of data. Adding context also means defining vocabulary. When asking students to find a *sum*, supplement the question with the terms *addition, altogether,* or *total.*

Above-grade-level students often already know the answers to the questions you ask. Answering these questions does not require much effort from these learners. Use the sentence stems below to create questions that will challenge these students.

- How many can you create…?
- What would happen if…?
- Defend the best use of…
- Evaluate your ideas…
- Judge your understanding of the problems…
- Debate whether or not…
- How can you improve…?
- Design a test that proves…

- What is the likelihood…?
- Predict the outcome…
- Form a hypothesis…
- What are three ways to classify…?
- Support your reason…
- Make a plan for…
- Propose a solution…
- What is an alternative to…?

Differentiation Strategies in This Book *(cont.)*

Multiple Intelligences

The multiple-intelligences model is based on the work of Howard Gardner (1983). He has identified nine intelligences, which include verbal/linguistic, logical/mathematical, visual/spatial, bodily/kinesthetic, musical/rhythmic, interpersonal, intrapersonal, naturalist, and existential. Gardner says that everyone possesses each of these intelligences, but in each of us, some intelligences are more developed than others.

Some research suggests that certain pathways of learning are stronger at certain stages of development. Sue Teele (1994) devised a survey titled the "Teele Inventory for Multiple Intelligences." She gave it to more than 6,000 students. Her research found that verbal/linguistic intelligence is strongest in kindergarten through third grade. It declines dramatically thereafter. The logical/mathematical intelligence is strongest in first through fourth grade. It also declines dramatically thereafter. The visual/spatial and bodily/kinesthetic intelligences were shown to be dominant throughout elementary and middle school. In addition, middle-school children also show a preference for musical/rhythmic and interpersonal intelligences. Teele's findings show that if elementary teachers want to use the best strategies, they must present lessons that incorporate verbal/linguistic, logical/mathematical, visual/spatial, and bodily/kinesthetic activities.

The Nine Multiple Intelligences

- The **Verbal/Linguistic** child thinks in words. This child likes to write, read, play word games, and tell interesting stories.

- The **Logical/Mathematical** child thinks by reasoning. This child likes finding solutions to problems, solving puzzles, experimenting, and calculating.

- The **Visual/Spatial** child thinks in pictures. This child likes to draw and design.

- The **Bodily/Kinesthetic** child thinks by using the body. This child likes dancing, moving, jumping, running, and touching.

- The **Musical/Rhythmic** child thinks in melodies and rhythms. This child likes listening to music, making music, tapping to the rhythm, and singing.

- The **Interpersonal** child thinks by talking about ideas with others. This child likes organizing events, being the leader, mediating between friends, and celebrating.

- The **Intrapersonal** child keeps thoughts to him- or herself. This child likes to set goals, meditate, daydream, and be in quiet places.

- The **Naturalist** child thinks by classifying. This child likes studying anything in nature, including rocks, animals, plants, and the weather.

- The **Existential** child reflects inwardly about the ultimate issues in life while learning and interacting with others. This child likes to express opinions.

Menu of Options

Providing students the opportunity to choose what activity they want to do increases their level of interest in what they are doing or learning. However, many students do not often get the chance to make choices about their work. It can be challenging and time-consuming for teachers to develop a variety of engaging activities. Yet offering options is essential to getting students interested and motivated in learning. When students are involved in something of their own choosing, they are more engaged in the learning process (Bess 1997; Brandt 1998).

Choices in the classroom can be offered in a variety of ways. Students can choose what they will learn (content), how they will learn (process), and how they will show what they have learned (product). A menu of options is a strategy that differentiates product by giving students the opportunity to choose from a list of highly engaging activities.

The menu of options strategy works well for many reasons. First, it operates much like a menu from a restaurant. A person looking at a menu sees all of the choices. Some cost more and some cost less. No one likes going to a restaurant and being told what to eat. People enjoy choosing what they prefer from the menu. In the same way, a menu of options offers students many different projects from which to choose. These projects are assigned various point values. The point values depend on the amount of work or detail involved in the project. Students must earn a set number of points determined by the teacher, but they can choose which activities they want to complete. Any kind of point system can be used. For example, basic projects that do not take much time can be worth 10 points. Projects that take a moderate amount of time and energy can be worth 30 points. Projects that are very time-consuming can be worth 50 points. If the students need to complete 80 points total, they can get to that total number in many different ways. They may choose a 50-point project and a 30-point project. Or, they may choose two 30-point projects and two 10-point projects.

Secondly, a menu of options is effective because the freedom of choice allows students to complete projects that are of interest to them. This increases the chance that the students will produce high-quality products. Students like to feel in control. When given a list from which to choose, students often choose projects that they like or that fit their learning styles. If the teacher provides enough variety, then all students can find projects that they feel passionate about.

As an alternative to creating a menu of options based on point systems, a teacher can create three or four sections on a menu of options and ask students to choose one project from each section. This strategy is helpful when there are a particular set of concepts that the teacher needs to be sure that students have learned.

Differentiation Strategies in This Book *(cont.)*

Choices Board

Everyone loves to make his or her own choices. Getting the chance to choose what we want increases the chances that we are actually interested in what we are doing or learning. Sadly, students do not always get the chance to make choices. Curriculum plans demand that teachers teach a certain way or about a certain topic. Students have to follow along and pretend to be interested. This does not fool most teachers. One key to getting students engaged in learning is to pique their interests by offering choices. It has been noted that when students are engaged in something of interest or choice, they are more engaged in the learning process (Bess 1997; Brandt 1998). Choices can be given in a variety of ways in a classroom. Choices can be given in what students will learn (content), how they will learn (process), and how they will show what they have learned (product).

Equally important is giving students academically appropriate assignments. Tiering or leveling assignments will ensure that students work on parallel tasks designed to have varied levels of depth, complexity, and abstractness along with varied degrees of scaffolding, support, and direction, depending on each student and the topic. All students work toward one goal, concept, or outcome, but the lesson is tiered to allow for different levels of readiness and performance. As students work, they build on their prior knowledge and understanding. Tiered assignments are productive because all students work on similar tasks that provide individual challenges. Students are motivated to be successful according to their own readiness levels as well as their own learning preferences.

Choices boards combine both choices and tiering by giving students the opportunities to choose leveled activities from a larger list. The difficulty levels of the activities vary.

△ above-grade-level students (shown by a triangle)

▢ on-grade-level students (shown by a square)

◯ below-grade-level students (shown by a circle)

☆ English language learners (shown by a star)

There should be at least two of each leveled activity so that students have an option. A teacher controls the levels of the activities, while students control which activity they will complete within that level. For example, when giving an on-grade-level student an assignment, the teacher may tell the student to choose any square activity from the choices board, and then challenge himself or herself by choosing a triangle activity.

Grouping Students

What Grouping Strategies Can I Use?

There are many variables that a teacher must consider when grouping students to create a successful learning environment. These variables include gender, chemistry between students, social maturity, academic readiness, and special needs. Some students will work well together while others will have great difficulty.

In this book, for ease of understanding, readiness levels are represented with a shape (triangle for above-grade level, square for on-grade level, and circle for below-grade level). In a classroom, however, a teacher might want to change the names for leveled groups from time to time. A teacher might use colors, animal names, or athletic team names to group students. For example, a teacher could cut out and distribute three different colors of construction paper squares, with each color representing a different readiness level. The teacher would tell all the "yellow square" students to find partners who also have a yellow square. This way, the teacher creates homogeneous groups while also allowing students to choose partners.

The following grouping strategies demonstrate various ways to group students in a differentiated classroom. This section is included so that you can learn to quickly group your students and easily apply the strategies.

Flexible Grouping

Flexible grouping means that members of a group change frequently. Routinely using the same grouping technique can lead to negative feelings, feelings of shame or a stigma associated with some group levels, lack of appropriate instruction, boredom, and behavior problems in the classroom. Flexible grouping can change the classroom environment daily, making it more interesting. It takes away the negative feelings and stigma of the struggling students because groups are always changing. No longer are the struggling students always in the same group.

Flexible grouping can occur within one lesson or over an entire unit. Try to modify groups from day to day, week to week, and unit to unit. Flexible grouping can include partner work, cooperative grouping, and whole-class grouping. Students' academic levels, interests, social chemistry, gender, or special needs can determine their placement in a particular group. Organize charts like the ones on the following pages to help you keep track of how you are grouping your students.

   © *Shell Education*

Grouping Students (cont.)

What Grouping Strategies Can I Use? (cont.)

Homogeneous Grouping

Homogeneous grouping brings together students who have the same readiness levels. It makes sense to group students homogeneously for reading groups and for language and mathematics skills lessons. To form groups, assess students' readiness levels in a content area. Then, order students from highest to lowest in readiness, and place them in order on a three-row horizontal grid.

One way to create homogeneous groups is by using the chart below. Notice that students in the same row have similar readiness levels.

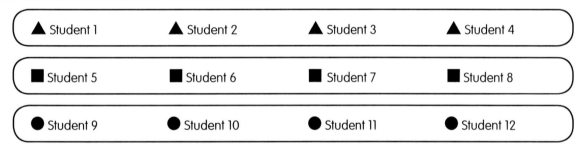

Homogeneous groups share similar readiness levels.

Heterogeneous Grouping

Heterogeneous grouping combines students with varied academic readiness levels. When grouping heterogeneously, look for some diversity in readiness and achievement levels so students can support one another as they learn together.

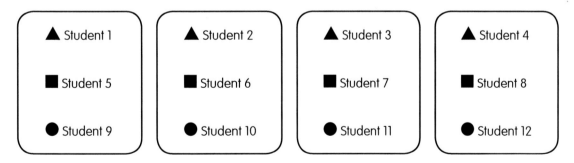

Heterogeneous groups have varying readiness levels.

Another strategy for heterogeneous grouping is to group by interest. Interest groups combine students with varied levels of achievement to create groups that have common interests. Other strategies for heterogeneous grouping include allowing students to self-select their groups, grouping by locality of seating arrangements in the classroom, and selecting groups at random.

What Grouping Strategies Can I Use? (cont.)

Flexogeneous Grouping

Flexogeneous grouping allows for the flexible grouping of homogeneous and heterogeneous groups within the same lesson. Students switch groups at least one time during the lesson to create another group. For example, the homogeneous groups meet for half the lesson and then switch to form heterogeneous groups for the rest of the lesson.

One easy flexogeneous grouping strategy is to jigsaw or mix up already established homogeneous groups. To jigsaw groups, allow homogeneous groups of students to work together for part of the lesson (circle, square, and triangle groups). Then, distinguish group members by labeling them *A*, *B*, and *C* within the same group. All of the *A*s form a new group, the *B*s form a new group, and the *C*s form a new group.

Homogeneous Groups   Heterogeneous Groups

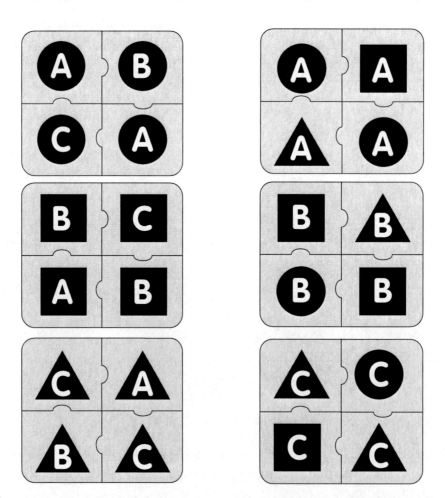

Flexogeneous grouping uses homogeneous and heterogeneous groups in a single lesson.

Working with English Language Learners

Strategies for Working with English Language Learners

Use visual media as an alternative to written responses. Have all students express their thinking through visual media, such as drawings, posters, or slide shows. This is an effective strategy for eliciting responses from English language learners. This also fosters creativity in all students, challenges above-grade-level students, provides opportunities for artistically inclined students who may struggle academically, and avoids singling out English language learners.

Frame questions to make the language accessible. At times, you will need to rephrase questions to clarify meaning for English language learners. Framing questions makes the language accessible to all students. Higher-order questions can be asked without reducing their rigor. Pose questions for English language learners with question stems or frames.

Example Question Stems/Frames

- What would happen if…?
- What is your opinion?
- Why do you think…?
- How would you prove…?
- Would it be better if…?

- How is _____ related to _____?
- If you could _____, what would you do?
- Can you invent _____?
- Why is _____ important?
- Why is _____ better than _____?

Give context to questions to enable understanding. This can be done by placing pictures or small icons directly next to key words. English language learners also benefit from chunking sentences. For example, with the question *In the ocean, how do wind and ocean currents make boats move?* English language learners can see right away that the question is about the ocean, so they have a context for answering the question.

Provide English language learners with sentence stems or frames to encourage higher-order thinking. These learners need language tools to help them express what they think. Sentence stems or frames will not only get the information you need and want from your English language learners, but it will also model how they should be speaking. You can provide these sentence stems or frames on small sticky notes for students to keep at their desks, or write them on laminated cards and distribute them to students, when necessary.

Example Sentence Stems/Frames

- This is important because…
- This is better because…
- This is similar because…
- This is different because…

- I agree with _____ because…
- I disagree with _____ because…
- I think _____ because…
- I think _____ will happen because…

Partner up, and let partners share aloud. Have English language learners work with language-proficient students to answer questions, solve problems, or create projects. Language-proficient partners can provide the academic vocabulary needed to express ideas. Prepare your language-proficient students to work with language learners by explaining that they must speak slowly and clearly and give these learners time to think and speak.

Working with English Language Learners *(cont.)*

How Can I Support English Language Learners?

All teachers should know the language-acquisition level of each of their English language learners. Knowing these levels will help to plan instruction. Using visuals to support oral and written language for students at Level 1 will help make the language more comprehensible. Students at Levels 2 and 3 benefit from pair work in speaking tasks, but they will need additional individual support during writing and reading tasks. Students at Levels 4 and 5 may still struggle with comprehending the academic language used during instruction, as well as with reading and writing. Use the chart below to plan appropriate questions and activities.

Proficiency Levels for English Language Learners—Quick Glance

Proficiency Level	Questions to Ask	Activities/Actions		
Level 1—Entering • minimal comprehension • no verbal production	• Where is…? • What is the main idea? • What examples do you see? • What are the parts of…? • What would happen if…? • What is your opinion?	• listen • point	• draw • circle	• mime
Level 2—Beginning • limited comprehension • short spoken phrases	• Can you list three…? • What facts or ideas show…? • What do the facts mean? • How is _____ related to _____? • Can you invent…? • Would it be better if…?	• move • match	• select • choose	• act/act out
Level 3—Developing • increased comprehension • simple sentences	• How did _____ happen? • Which is your best answer? • What questions would you ask about…? • Why do you think…? • If you could _____ , what would you do? • How would you prove…?	• name • label • tell/say	• list • categorize	• respond (with 1–2 words) • group
Level 4—Expanding • very good comprehension • some errors in speech	• How would you show…? • How would you summarize…? • What would result if…? • What is the relationship between…? • What is an alternative to…? • Why is this important?	• recall • compare/contrast • describe	• retell • explain • role-play	• define • summarize • restate
Level 5—Bridging • comprehension comparable to native English speakers • speaks using complex sentences	• How would you describe…? • What is meant by…? • How would you use…? • What ideas justify…? • What is an original way to show…? • Why is it better that…?	• analyze • evaluate • create	• defend • justify • express	• complete • support

How to Use This Book

Teacher Lesson Plans

Each lesson is presented in a straightforward, step-by-step format so that teachers can easily implement it right away.

Differentiation Strategies are highlighted for quick reference.

Standards are aligned to grade-level content and English language learner needs.

Materials lists outline items needed for each lesson. If lessons call for slide show software, you might use *Microsoft Powerpoint*® or *Prezi*®. Additional resources are listed on page 167.

English Language Support suggestions offer ideas for adapting and customizing the lesson.

Anchor Activities extend the lesson and promote further investigation and practice for students who finish early.

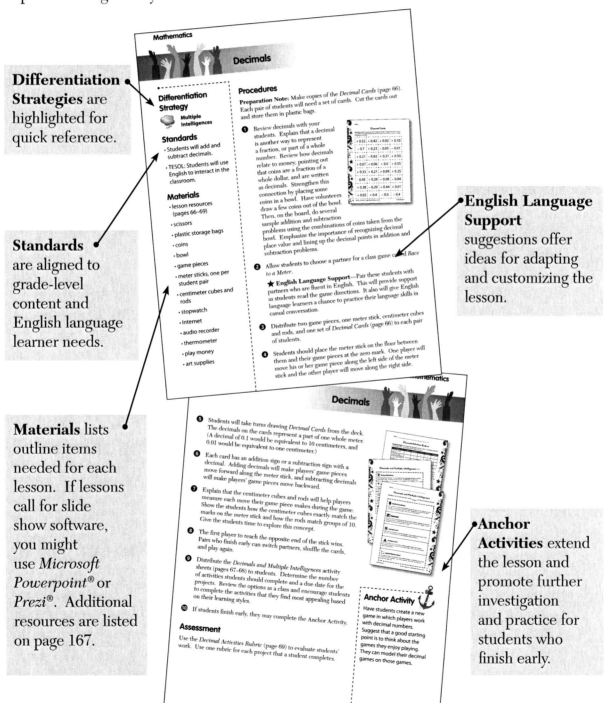

How to Use This Book *(cont.)*

Lesson Resources

These pages include student reproducibles and teacher resources needed to implement each lesson.

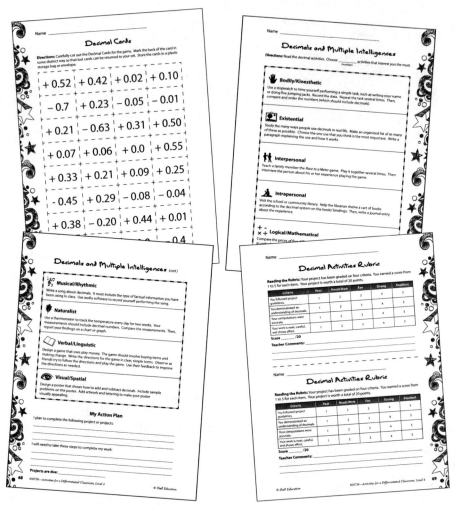

Teacher Resource CD

Helpful reproducibles and images are provided on the accompanying CD. Find a detailed listing of the CD contents on page 168.

- JPEGs of all photographs
- Reproducible PDFs of all student activity sheets and teacher resource pages
- Reproducible PDFs of blank graphic organizers
- Answer key

Correlations to Standards

Shell Education is committed to producing educational materials that are research and standards based. In this effort, we have correlated all of our products to the academic standards of all 50 states, the District of Columbia, and the Department of Defense Dependent Schools.

How to Find Standards Correlations

To print a customized correlation report of this product for your state, visit our website at **http://www.shelleducation.com** and follow the on-screen directions. If you require assistance in printing correlation reports, please contact Customer Service at 1-877-777-3450.

Purpose and Intent of Standards

The No Child Left Behind (NCLB) legislation mandates that all states adopt academic standards that identify the skills students will learn in kindergarten through grade 12. While many states had already adopted academic standards prior to NCLB, the legislation set requirements to ensure the standards were detailed and comprehensive.

Standards are designed to focus instruction and guide adoption of curricula. Standards are statements that describe the criteria necessary for students to meet specific academic goals. They define the knowledge, skills, and content students should acquire at each level. Standards are also used to develop standardized tests to evaluate students' academic progress.

Teachers are required to demonstrate how their lessons meet state standards. State standards are used in the development of all of our products, so educators can be assured that they meet the academic requirements of each state.

McREL Compendium

We use the Mid-continent Research for Education and Learning (McREL) Compendium to create standards correlations. Each year, McREL analyzes state standards and revises the compendium. By following this procedure, McREL is able to produce a general compilation of national standards. Each lesson in this product is based on one or more McREL standards. The chart on page 20 lists each standard taught in this book and the page numbers for the corresponding lessons.

TESOL Standards

The lessons in this book promote English language development for English language learners. The standards listed on page 21, from the Teachers of English to Speakers of Other Languages (TESOL) Association, support the language objectives presented throughout the lessons.

Correlations to Standards *(cont.)*

	McREL Standards	Lesson Title	Page
Language Arts	Language Arts 7.2, Level I: Students will understand the main idea and supporting details of simple expository information.	Main Idea and Supporting Details	40
	Language Arts 1.3, Level II: Students will use strategies to edit and publish written work.	Self-Editing	22
	Language Arts 1.8, Level II: Students will write narrative accounts, such as poems and stories.	Haiku Poetry	52
	Language Arts 3.11, Level II: Students will use conventions of punctuation in written compositions.	Writing Dialogue	28
	Language Arts 6.3, Level II: Students will understand the basic concept of plot.	Story Elements	46
	Language Arts 7.5, Level II: Students will summarize and paraphrase information in texts.	Summarizing	34
Mathematics	Mathematics 2.4, Level II: Students will understand the basic meaning of place value.	Number Sense	58
	Mathematics 2.5, Level II: Students will understand the concepts related to fractions and decimals.	Fractions	76
	Mathematics 3.2, Level II: Students will add and subtract decimals.	Decimals	64
	Mathematics 4.4, Level II: Students will understand relationships between measures, such as area and perimeter.	Perimeter and Area	82
	Mathematics 5.5, Level II: Students will use motion geometry, such as turns, flips, and slides, to understand geometric relationships.	Geometric Transformations	88
	Mathematics 6.4, Level II: Students will organize and display data in simple bar graphs.	Measuring and Graphing	70
Science	Science 1.1, Level II: Students will understand that water exists in the air in different forms and changes from one form to another through various processes.	The Water Cycle and Weather	94
	Science 2.1, Level II: Students will understand how features on Earth's surface are constantly changed by a combination of slow and rapid processes.	Erosion	124
	Science 3.2, Level II: Students will know that Earth is one of several planets that orbit the sun and that the moon orbits Earth.	The Moon	100
	Science 5.1, Level II: Students will understand that animals progress through life cycles of birth, growth and development, reproduction, and death; the details of these life cycles are different for different organisms.	Life Cycles	112
	Science 6.3, Level II: Students will understand that an organism's patterns of behavior are related to the nature of that organism's environment.	Animal Adaptations	118
	Science 8.1, Level II: Students will understand that matter has different states and that each state has distinct physical properties; some common materials such as water can be changed from one state to another by heating or cooling.	States of Matter	106
Social Studies	Economics 3.3, Level II: Students will understand that businesses are willing and able to sell more of a product when its price goes up and less when its price goes down.	Supply and Demand	154
	Geography 1.1, Level II: Students will understand the basic elements of maps and globes.	Map Skills	130
	History 3.10, Level II: Students will understand how the ideas of significant people affected the history of the state.	History's Heroes	148
	History 7.2, Level II: Students will understand the effects geography has had on the different aspects of societies.	American Indians and the Environment	136
	History 7.7, Level II: Students will understand European explorers of the fifteenth and sixteenth centuries, their reasons for exploring, the information gained from their journeys, and what happened as a result of their travels.	The Age of Exploration	142
	History 17.2, Level II: Students will understand the major responsibilities of the legislative, executive, and judicial branches of their state government.	State Government	160

Correlations to Standards *(cont.)*

	TESOL Standard	Lesson Title	Page
TESOL 2.1	Students will use English to interact in the classroom.	Writing Dialogue	28
		Summarizing	34
		Main Idea and Supporting Details	40
		Number Sense	58
		Decimals	64
		Perimeter and Area	82
		Geometric Transformations	88
		The Water Cycle and Weather	94
		Supply and Demand	154
TESOL 2.2	Students will use English to obtain, process, construct, and provide subject matter information in spoken and written form.	Self-Editing	22
		The Moon	100
		States of Matter	106
		Life Cycles	112
TESOL 2.3	Students will use appropriate learning strategies to construct and apply academic knowledge.	Story Elements	46
		Measuring and Graphing	70
		Fractions	76
		Animal Adaptations	118
		Map Skills	130
		The Age of Exploration	142
		History's Heroes	148
		State Government	160
TESOL 3.1	Students will use the appropriate language variety, register, and genre according to audience, purpose, and setting.	Haiku Poetry	52
TESOL 3.2	Students will use nonverbal communication appropriate to audience, purpose, and setting.	American Indians and the Environment	136
TESOL 3.3	Students will use appropriate learning strategies to extend their sociolinguistic and sociocultural competence.	Erosion	124

Language Arts

Self-Editing

Differentiation Strategy

 Leveled Questions

Standards

- Students will use strategies to edit and publish written work.

- TESOL: Students will use English to obtain, process, construct, and provide subject matter information in spoken and written form.

Materials

- lesson resources (pages 24–27)

- ingredients for making a familiar snack

- utensils for assembling a familiar snack

- art supplies

Procedures

1. Demonstrate for the class how to make a familiar snack, such as a peanut butter and jelly sandwich, a sundae, or s'mores. As you work, explain each step aloud. Do not assume that everyone knows how to make the snack.

2. Have students return to their desks. Ask them to write a paragraph explaining in their own words how to make the snack.

3. After students have finished their paragraphs, write the acronym *CUPS* on the board. Introduce this four-step process for editing. Explain that *C* stands for *capitalization*. During the first step of editing, students should check their work for capitalization errors. *U* stands for *understanding*. During the second step, students should make sure their writing makes sense. *P* stands for *punctuation*. During the third step, students will check their work for punctuation errors. *S* stands for *spelling*. During the final step, students will check their spelling. Ask students to record the steps in *CUPS* on their papers.

4. Invite students to each choose a partner for the next activity.

   ★ **English Language Support**—Encourage English language learners to choose language-proficient partners with whom they feel comfortable taking academic risks. In addition, take time to explain to their partners the best ways to work with English language learners. Ask them to speak clearly and slowly, point to text as they read, and allow extra time for them to answer questions.

5. Have students read their paragraphs aloud to their partners. Ask students to circle each punctuation mark in their own writing. Next, have them check to make sure that a capital letter follows every punctuation mark that ends a sentence. Ask students to fix capitalization errors before moving on to the next step.

6. Have students silently reread their paragraphs. Ask them to make sure they make sense and follow a logical sequence. Have students point out any confusing parts of their partners' writing. Allow students time to make necessary corrections.

© *Shell Education*

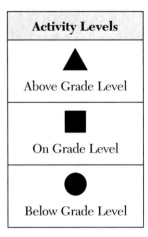

Self-Editing

7 Students should read the paragraphs again, this time checking for punctuation. Explain that when they see a period or ending punctuation, they should pause and silently count to three. If they do not see ending punctuation, they are not allowed to pause, even for a breath! This will help students identify run-on sentences. Ask them to fix these sentence errors before moving on to the next step.

8 Have students reread their paragraphs. The next activity will help students identify spelling errors. Ask students to start with the last word of their paragraphs and silently read from end to beginning. Reading backwards will slow students down and keep them from skimming. Spelling errors should jump out at them. Ask students to fix the spelling errors before moving on to the next step.

9 Finally, students should read their paragraphs aloud to their partners one last time.

10 Distribute the *Self-Editing Practice* activity sheet (pages 24–26) to students according to their readiness levels. Have students complete the activity sheet according to the directions.

11 The *Self-Editing Extension* activity sheet (page 27) is a fun way to extend the lesson. Have students work independently, or in groups, to complete one of the projects. The goal is for students to help one another commit the *CUPS* method to memory.

12 If students finish early, they may complete the Anchor Activity.

Assessment

Review students' responses to the leveled questions to evaluate their understanding of the concept.

Activity Levels
▲
Above Grade Level
■
On Grade Level
●
Below Grade Level

Anchor Activity

Have students set up a *CUPS* self-editing station in the classroom. Have them stock it with editing pens, sticky notes, and laminated posters explaining the steps of the *CUPS* method. Train some of these students to be *CUPS* experts. Assign them the job of keeping the station neat and well stocked. These students could also keep "office hours" at the station to help classmates as they edit their work. Provide time for students to visit the station before handing in written assignments.

Name _____

Self-Editing Practice

Part 1 Directions: Write at least one paragraph about a time you were surprised.

_____
_____
_____
_____
_____
_____
_____
_____
_____

Part 2 Directions: Now, use the *CUPS* method you learned in class to edit your paragraph. Check your Capitalization, Understanding, Punctuation, and Spelling.

Part 3 Directions: Answer the questions about self-editing.

1. How effective is the *CUPS* method for improving your writing? Explain.

_____
_____
_____
_____
_____
_____
_____

2. How could you teach the *CUPS* method to other students? Design a lesson and describe your idea below.

_____
_____
_____
_____
_____
_____
_____
_____

 © *Shell Education*

Name _____

Self-Editing Practice

Part 1 Directions: Write a paragraph about a time you were surprised.

_____

_____

_____

_____

_____

_____

_____

_____

Part 2 Directions: Choose a partner with a square at the top of his or her activity sheet. Then, work together to edit each other's paragraphs. Use the *CUPS* method you learned in class.

Step 1: Check for *Capitalization* errors.

Step 2: Check for *Understanding*. Does it make sense?

Step 3: Check for *Punctuation* errors.

Step 4: Check for *Spelling* errors.

Part 3 Directions: Answer the questions about self-editing.

1. Which step of the *CUPS* method is hardest for you? Explain why.

_____

_____

_____

_____

2. Can you create a mnemonic device (memory tool) that will help other students recall the steps of the *CUPS* method? Write it on the lines below.

_____

_____

_____

_____

_____

Name _____

Self-Editing Practice

Part 1 Directions: Read the paragraph below about a surprise. You should notice some errors as you read.

We were all surprised when the lights whent out. Lightning was crashing all around us rain was pooring down outside? we could hear the hard rain drops pinging on the windows. Everyone knew this storm was probably going to last most of the night. i decided to look for a flashlight under the kitchen sink sally went to look for matches and canddles in the closet. We kept telling ourselves not too panic. The weather chunnel said it was going to storm.

Part 2 Directions: Choose a partner with a circle at the top of his or her activity sheet. Edit the paragraph together. Make corrections in pen. Use the *CUPS* method you learned in class to find all 12 mistakes.

　　Step 1: Check for <u>C</u>apitalization errors. *(Hint: There are 3 errors.)*

　　Step 2: Check for <u>U</u>nderstanding. Is the story in the right order? *(Hint: There is 1 error.)*

　　Step 3: Check for <u>P</u>unctuation errors. Are there run-on sentences?
　　　　　　(Hint: There are 3 errors.)

　　Step 4: Check for <u>S</u>pelling errors. *(Hint: There are 5 errors.)*

Part 3 Directions: Answer the questions about self-editing.

1. Which step of the *CUPS* method is most important? Explain why.

　　_____

　　_____

　　_____

2. How would you explain the *CUPS* method to a friend? Write your description below.

　　_____

　　_____

　　_____

　　_____

　　_____

　　_____

Name _____

Self-Editing Extension

The *CUPS* method is a great way to catch your own writing mistakes, but it only works if you can remember all of the steps and how to do them.

Directions: The projects below are designed to help you and your classmates memorize the *CUPS* method. Choose one of the projects to complete.

Project due date: _____

Sing a Silly Song

Have you ever had a song stuck in your head? Music is a great memory tool. Choose a familiar tune. Then, make up new words that explain the *CUPS* method. Be prepared to teach the song to your classmates.

Paint a Poster

Catch your classmates' attention with a colorful poster. Spell out the *CUPS* method in bold, bright letters. Make sure you explain each step and how to do it. Illustrations and symbols will make your poster a great classroom resource. The final product should be neat, clear, and visually appealing.

Act It Out

If you really want your classmates to remember *CUPS*, perform a skit that explains the method. Make your play silly, dramatic, or both, but be sure it holds your classmates' attention. Costumes and props will make it even more memorable.

Make It a Game

Use the *CUPS* method as inspiration for a game. Design and make a board game, card game, or any other type of game that helps teach self-editing skills. Borrow ideas from your favorite games and combine them into something new and exciting. Make a final product that your classmates can play.

Writing Dialogue

Differentiation Strategy

 Menu of Options

Standards

- Students will use conventions of punctuation in written compositions.

- TESOL: Students will use English to interact in the classroom.

Materials

- lesson resources (pages 30–33)

- novels and chapter books *(See page 167.)*

- sticky notes

- newspapers

- magazines

- glue

- scissors

Procedures

1 Engage students by reading an interesting conversation aloud from a popular novel. After reading, ask students to describe the type of passage you read. Then, explain that when characters speak out loud, their words are called *dialogue*. Authors put quotation marks around dialogue to signal to readers that the words are being said out loud. Challenge students to browse chapter books for examples of dialogue to share with classmates. Provide sticky notes for them to mark examples.

2 Instruct students to carefully examine the dialogue examples they found. Ask them to notice where the punctuation marks are in relation to the quotation marks. Have them identify what usually follows words spoken out loud. Ask them about the use of capital letters in dialogue.

3 Display the *How to Write Dialogue* example (page 30) to the class. Review each rule and its example(s). Have students check the dialogue examples in their novels to see the rules in action.

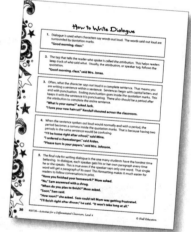

4 Have students play a game called *Table Talk* to practice writing dialogue. Instruct students to move their desks together into small groups of four or five. Each student will need two or three sheets of lined paper. Tell students that for this game, note passing is encouraged! In fact, it is the only way they will be able to communicate. The catch is that every note must be written in the form of dialogue. For example, *"What did you do yesterday after school?" asked Mrs. Jones. "I went to a swim meet," said Bailey.* Students will write notes to group members and respond to the notes they are given.

★ **English Language Support**—Provide a sheet of sample sentences for your English language learners to copy into their *Table Talk* notes if they get stuck. These should be questions and statements that students would want to write to their peers.

Writing Dialogue

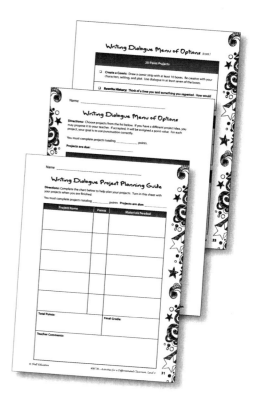

5 Highlight the following rules for students before *Table Talk* begins:

- All notes must be school appropriate.

- Students must respond to every note, as time allows.

- Notes may be passed among group members only.

- The teacher has the right to read notes to check for punctuation and subject matter.

6 After the game, distribute the *Writing Dialogue Menu of Options* activity sheets (pages 32–33) to students. Explain to students that they will complete several of the listed activities. They may also choose to propose additional or alternative projects for your approval. Review the options with the class. Decide ahead of time the number of points students need to complete from the menu, and determine a due date. Have students complete the *Writing Dialogue Project Planning Guide* activity sheet (page 31) to assure that they are planning to complete enough projects to meet the point requirement.

7 If students finish early, they may complete the Anchor Activity.

Assessment

Use the student project planning guide to record each student's grades. Total up the amount of points the student earned. Decide on a grading scale. Provide meaningful comments about each student's projects so he or she can have feedback on his or her work.

Anchor Activity

Have students create posters for the classroom that explain the rules of writing dialogue and give examples of them. Provide poster board and coloring supplies at a station. Remind students that the text on posters must be large, neat, and spelled correctly. Any artwork added to the design should enhance the message rather than distract from it.

How to Write Dialogue

1. Dialogue is used when characters say words out loud. The words said out loud are surrounded by quotation marks.

   "Good morning, class."

2. The tag that tells the reader who spoke is called the *attribution*. This helps readers keep track of who said what. Usually, the attribution, or speaker tag, follows the quotation.

   "Good morning, class," said Mrs. Jones.

3. Often, what the character says out loud is a complete sentence. That means you are writing a sentence within a sentence. Sentences begin with capital letters and end with punctuation. Ending punctuation goes inside the quotation marks. This keeps it with the sentence it is punctuating. There also should be a period after the attribution to complete the entire sentence.

   "What is your name?" asked Jack.

   "I love your new haircut!" Kendall shouted across the classroom.

4. When the sentence spoken out loud would normally end with a period, the period becomes a comma inside the quotation marks. That is because having two periods in the same sentence would be confusing.

   "I'll be home right after school," said Mina.

   "I ordered a cheeseburger," said Aiden.

   "Please turn in your papers," said Mrs. Johnson.

5. The final rule for writing dialogue is the one many students have the hardest time believing. In dialogue, each speaker gets his or her own paragraph every time he or she speaks. This is true even if the speaker says only one word. That single word will get a paragraph of its own! This formatting makes it much easier for readers to follow conversations in print.

   "Have you finished your homework?" Mom asked.

   "No," Sam answered with a shrug.

   "When do you plan to finish?" Mom asked.

   "Soon," Sam said.

   "How soon?" she asked. Sam could tell Mom was getting frustrated.

   "I'll finish right after dinner," he said. "It won't take long at all."

Name _____

Writing Dialogue Project Planning Guide

Directions: Complete the chart below to help plan your projects. Turn in this sheet with your projects when you are finished.

You must complete projects totaling _____ points. **Projects are due:** _____

Project Name	Points	Materials Needed
Total Points:		**Final Grade:**
Teacher Comments:		

Name _____

Writing Dialogue Menu of Options

Directions: Choose projects from the list below. If you have a different project idea, you may propose it to your teacher. If accepted, it will be assigned a point value. For each project, your goal is to use punctuation correctly.

You must complete projects totaling _____ points.

Projects are due: _____

50-Point Projects
❑ **Interview:** Interview a member of your family about his or her favorite hobby. Ask 10 questions. Write the interview questions and the answers in the form of dialogue.
❑ **Create a Conversation:** Cut out a picture of people from a magazine or newspaper. Imagine the conversation the people might be having. Give the people names. Then, write the dialogue. You must write at least 15 sentences of dialogue.
❑ **Become an Author:** Check out a wordless picture book from the library. Write a story to go along with the illustrations. Be sure to use at least seven lines of dialogue.

30-Point Projects
❑ **Order Takeout:** Pretend that you called a pizza restaurant to place an order. Write the conversation between you and the person at the restaurant. The conversation should be at least 10 sentences long.
❑ **Write the Rules:** Think of a game you know how to play. How would you explain the rules? Write the instructions for the game in the form of a dialogue between you and a friend.

Writing Dialogue Menu of Options *(cont.)*

20-Point Projects

❑ **Create a Comic:** Draw a comic strip with at least 10 boxes. Be creative with your characters, setting, and plot. Use dialogue in at least seven of the boxes.

❑ **Rewrite History:** Think of a time when you said something you regretted. How would you change your words if you could? Write the conversation, but change your words to what you *should* have said.

10-Point Projects

❑ **Newspaper Collage:** Find 10 examples of dialogue in a newspaper. Cut them out and glue them to a piece of construction paper.

❑ **Book Hunt:** Find five examples of dialogue in chapter books. Write down the book titles, authors' names, and the examples of dialogue. Be sure to copy sentences carefully.

Student-Proposed Projects

❑ _____

_____

_____

_____

❑ _____

_____

_____

_____

Summarizing

Differentiation Strategy

 Tiered Graphic Organizers

Standards

- Students will summarize and paraphrase information in texts.

- TESOL: Students will use English to interact in the classroom.

Materials

- lesson resources (pages 36–39)

- an episode of a children's television show

- age-appropriate picture books *(See page 167.)*

Procedures

Preparation Note: Bring in an episode of a popular children's television show for students to view. You could check out a DVD from your local library, rent a DVD from a video store, or download an episode from the Internet. The episode should be no longer than 30 minutes.

1 Begin the lesson by gauging students' knowledge of summarizing. Remind them that a summary is a short recap of the main events in a story. Nonessential details must be left out. Explain that every summary has a beginning, a middle, and an end. Summaries name the main characters and describe the most important events. On the board, sketch a simple three-column chart. Label the sections *Beginning*, *Middle*, and *End*.

2 Have each student take out a sheet of paper. Students should divide their papers into three sections vertically. Have them label the sections *Beginning*, *Middle*, and *End*.

3 Tell students that they will watch an episode of a television show. As they watch, they should try to identify the main events that happen in the beginning, middle, and end of the episode.

4 After the show, ask students to complete their charts. They should write what happens in the beginning, middle, and end of the episode. Students should include the names of the main characters and descriptions of the most important events.

★ **English Language Support**—Instead of having English language learners write their ideas, bring them together in a group for a discussion. Have them work together to orally summarize the beginning, middle, and end of the episode.

5 Allow time for the whole class to share and compare their summaries. Discuss which details must be included and which should be left out.

Summarizing

6 Distribute the *Summary Practice* activity sheets (pages 36–38) according to the readiness levels of students. In addition, distribute the *The Princess and the Pea* activity sheet (page 39) to below-grade-level students. Circulate and assist, as necessary.

Activity Levels
▲
Above Grade Level
■
On Grade Level
●
Below Grade Level

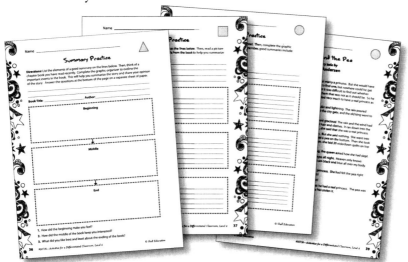

7 If students finish early, they may complete the Anchor Activity.

Assessment

Assess students' understanding by grading their graphic organizers.

Anchor Activity

Have students complete a novel-summary graphic organizer. Prepare a five-row by five-column chart that fills a sheet of paper. Distribute this graphic organizer to students as they begin reading a new novel. Explain that after they finish reading the first chapter, they should write a short summary of the events in the first box of the chart. The summary must fit in the box. Students should repeat this activity for every chapter.

Name _____

Summary Practice

Directions: List the elements of a good summary on the lines below. Then, think of a chapter book that you have recently read. Complete the graphic organizer to outline the important events in the book. This will help you summarize the story and share your opinion of the story. Answer the questions at the bottom of the page on a separate sheet of paper.

_____

_____

Book Title: _____ **Author:** _____

> **Beginning**
>
>
>
>
>

↓

> **Middle**
>
>
>
>
>

↓

> **End**
>
>
>
>
>

1. How does the beginning make you feel?

2. How does the middle of the book keep you interested?

3. What do you like best and least about the ending of the book?

Summary Practice

Directions: List the elements of a good summary on the lines below. Then, read a picture book. Complete the graphic organizer using details from the book to help you summarize the story.

A good summary includes: _____
_____

Book Title: _____

Author: _____

Beginning

_____
_____
_____
_____
_____

↓

Middle

_____
_____
_____
_____
_____

↓

End

_____
_____
_____
_____
_____

Name _____

Summary Practice

Directions: Read *The Princess and the Pea* activity sheet. Then, complete the graphic organizer. It will help you summarize the story. Remember, good summaries include:

- the names of main characters
- descriptions of important events
- a beginning, a middle, and an end

Passage Title: _____

Author: _____

Beginning
_____
_____
_____
_____
_____

Middle
_____
_____
_____
_____
_____

End
_____
_____
_____
_____
_____

Name _____

The Princess and the Pea

Based on the fairy tale by
Hans Christian Andersen

Once upon a time, there was a prince who wanted to marry a princess. But she would have to be a real princess. He traveled all over the world to find one, but nowhere could he get what he wanted. There were enough princesses, but it was difficult to find out whether they were real. There was always something about them that was not as it should be. So he came home again and was sad, for he would have liked very much to have a real princess as his bride.

One evening, a terrible storm came. There was thunder and lightning. The rain poured down in torrents. Suddenly, a knocking was heard at the city gate, and the old king went to open it.

It was a princess standing there in the storm. Good gracious! The rain and the wind had made her quite a sight. The water ran down from her hair and clothes. It ran down into the toes of her shoes and out again at the heels. And yet, she said that she was a real princess.

"Well, we'll soon find that out," thought the old queen. But she said nothing. She went into the bedroom, took all the bedding off the bed, and laid a pea on the bottom. Then she took 20 mattresses and laid them on the pea. On top of that, she laid 20 eiderdown quilts on top of the mattresses.

The princess had to lie all night on this. In the morning, the queen asked how she had slept.

"Oh, very badly!" said she. "I have scarcely closed my eyes all night. Heaven only knows what was in the bed! I was lying on something hard. I am black and blue all over my body. It's horrible!"

Now the king and queen knew that this girl was a real princess. She had felt the pea right through the 20 mattresses and the 20 eiderdown quilts!

Nobody but a real princess could be as sensitive as that!

So the prince took her for his wife, for now he knew that he had a real princess. The pea was put in the museum, where it may still be seen, if no one has stolen it.

Main Idea and Supporting Details

Differentiation Strategy

  Tiered Assignments

Standards

- Students will understand the main idea and supporting details of simple expository information.
- TESOL: Students will use English to interact in the classroom.

Materials

- lesson resources (pages 42–45)
- index cards
- ruler
- scissors
- one hole punch
- markers or crayons
- clothing hangers
- yarn, string, or ribbon

Procedures

❶ Place students in heterogeneous groups of four or five students. Ask them to make a list of three things every member of the group has in common. Encourage them to avoid obvious traits, such as being in the same grade or the same class. For example, a group's list might include the following: *We all like funny movies. We have all traveled outside of the United States. We all have pets.*

❷ Allow time for groups to share their lists with the class.

❸ Model for students how to support their main ideas with details. Explain that these are called *supporting details*. Their job is to give more information about the main idea. For example, to support the main idea that group members all like funny movies, one supporting detail might be that they all liked a popular movie that just came out in their area.

❹ Ask students to write three supporting details for each of their three main ideas. Circulate and assist as needed.

❺ Have students make mobiles to display their main ideas and supporting details. Distribute six index cards to each group. Have groups write and illustrate their three main ideas on three separate index cards. Then, have them cut the rest of the index cards into three equal pieces. On those small cards, have groups write and illustrate each of their three supporting details.

❻ Have students punch holes in the top-middle of each card. They should also punch three holes across the bottoms of each main idea card. Distribute one hanger and several pieces of yarn or ribbon to each group. Show students how to tie the main ideas to the hangers and the supporting details to the main-idea cards. Hang the mobiles from the classroom ceiling.

Main Idea and Supporting Details

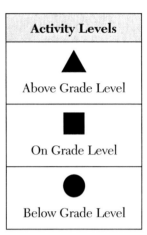

7 Distribute the *Main Idea and Supporting Details Practice* activity sheets (pages 42–44) to students based on their readiness levels.

★ **English Language Support**—Choose the activity sheet that best meets the needs of the English language learners. Work with them in a small group as they complete the sheet. Review and explain vocabulary words, as needed. If necessary, allow them to give verbal answers while you take notes.

8 If students finish early, they may complete the Anchor Activity.

Assessment

Distribute the *Main Idea and Supporting Details Assessment* activity sheet (page 45) to students to evaluate how well they are able to determine the main idea and supporting details of a paragraph. Use the following questions to evaluate the graphic organizers students create. If answers to all questions are *yes*, then students have mastered the objective of this lesson. For students who do not get all *yes* answers, review the concepts missed and reassess.

- *Did the student design a graphic organizer?*
- *Did the student identify the main idea?*
- *Did the student identify three supporting details?*

Activity Levels
▲
Above Grade Level
■
On Grade Level
●
Below Grade Level

Anchor Activity

Have students write a short narrative or expository essay. Fill a cup with slips of paper labeled with topic ideas, such as *The Best Trip Ever*, *My Pet*, *My Best Friend*, *A Great Day*, *Soccer*, *Video Games*, *Siblings*, and *School Lunches*. Students can select an essay topic by pulling a slip from the cup. Remind students that they must write a main idea and at least three supporting details. Then, have students trade essays with classmates and try to identify the main idea and supporting details.

Name _____

Main Idea and Supporting Details Practice

Part 1 Directions: Read the supporting details. Then, write a main idea that fits the details.

1. **Supporting Details**

   a. Laurie tells people's secrets.

   b. Laurie says mean things to her friends.

   c. Laurie never shares her school supplies with classmates.

   Main Idea: _____

2. **Supporting Details**

   a. Ahmed can outrun the other kids on his baseball team.

   b. Ahmed hits a home run almost every game.

   c. Ahmed has a fast pitch.

   Main Idea: _____

Part 2 Directions: Read the main idea. Then, write supporting details to give more information about the main idea. Be creative with the details you add.

3. **Main Idea:** Isabella had the best birthday ever!

   Supporting Details

   a. _____

   b. _____

   c. _____

4. **Main Idea:** It was very hot last summer.

   Supporting Details

   a. _____

   b. _____

   c. _____

Part 3 Directions: Now write your own main idea and supporting details.

5. **Main Idea:** _____

   Supporting Details

   a. _____

   b. _____

   c. _____

Name _____

Main Idea and Supporting Details Practice

Part 1 Directions: Read the supporting details. Then, write a main idea that fits the details. For numbers 3 and 4, add a supporting detail as well.

1. **Supporting Details**

   a. Laurie tells people's secrets.

   b. Laurie says mean things to her friends.

   c. Laurie never shares her school supplies with classmates.

   Main Idea: _____

2. **Supporting Details**

   a. Ahmed can outrun the other kids on his baseball team.

   b. Ahmed hits a home run almost every game.

   c. Ahmed has a fast pitch.

   Main Idea: _____

3. **Supporting Details**

   a. All of Isabella's friends came to her birthday party.

   b. They played games and ate pizza and cupcakes.

   c. _____

   Main Idea: _____

4. **Supporting Details**

   a. We had to use the air conditioner almost every day last summer.

   b. We drank lots of cold water and ate ice pops to stay cool.

   c. _____

   Main Idea: _____

Part 2 Directions: Read the main idea. Then, write supporting details to give more information about the main idea. Be creative with the details you add.

5. **Supporting Details**

   a. _____

   b. _____

   c. _____

   Main Idea: Winter is my favorite season.

Name _____

Main Idea and Supporting Details Practice

Part 1 Directions: Read the supporting details. Then, complete the main idea statement. Make sure the main idea fits the details.

1. **Supporting Details**

   a. Laurie tells people's secrets.

   b. Laurie says mean things to her friends.

   c. Laurie never shares her school supplies with classmates.

   Main Idea: Laurie is _____

2. **Supporting Details**

   a. Ahmed can outrun the other kids on his baseball team.

   b. Ahmed hits a home run almost every game.

   c. Ahmed has a fast pitch.

   Main Idea: Ahmed is _____

3. **Supporting Details**

   a. All of Isabella's friends came to her birthday party.

   b. They played games and ate pizza and cupcakes.

   c. Isabella loved all of the gifts her friends gave her.

   Main Idea: Isabella had _____

4. **Supporting Details**

   a. We had to use the air conditioner almost every day last summer.

   b. We drank lots of cold water and ate ice pops to stay cool.

   c. We went to the pool a lot.

   Main Idea: Last summer was _____

Part 2 Directions: Read the main idea. Then, write supporting details to give more information about the main idea. Be creative with the details you add.

5. **Supporting Details**

   a. I love to go sledding.

   b. _____

   c. _____

   Main Idea: Winter is my favorite season.

Name _____

Main Idea and Supporting Details Assessment

Directions: Read the paragraph below. Then, use the space below to design your own graphic organizer to help you visually record the main idea and at least three supporting details. Use the criteria checklist at the bottom of the page to make sure you have included all of the necessary information.

> The world's first postage stamp was called the Penny Black. It was introduced on May 1, 1840, in Great Britain and Ireland. It cost only a penny! It was a black and white stamp with a picture of the British queen on it. A blue two-penny stamp with the same picture came out a few days later. The blue stamp was for mail that weighed more. Before the postage stamp, people paid for their letters and packages with cash when they were delivered.

Criteria Checklist

☐ Did you design a graphic organizer?

☐ Did you identify the main idea?

☐ Did you identify three supporting details?

Story Elements

Differentiation Strategy

 Choices Board

Standards

- Students will understand the basic concept of plot.
- TESOL: Students will use appropriate learning strategies to construct and apply academic knowledge.

Materials

- lesson resources (pages 48–51)
- chart paper and markers
- timer
- books of fairy tales (*See page 167.*)
- slide show software
- Internet
- index cards
- art supplies
- sentence strips
- art books (*optional*)

Procedures

Preparation Note: Before class begins, place students in heterogeneous groups of five or six. Arrange students' desks in vertical rows, with one row for each group. Group members should sit behind one another in any order.

★ **English Language Support**—Place English language learners in each of the groups. If necessary, partner each English language learner with a language-proficient student in the group. Take time to explain to the language-proficient students the best ways to work with English language learners. Ask them to speak clearly and slowly, to point to the text as they read aloud, and to ask for and listen patiently to their ideas.

❶ Explain to students that they will be working together to write 25 (*or however many students are in the class*) stories in one day! They will do this by passing their stories from person to person within their groups. Each person will add on to every other person's story.

❷ Review the story elements of setting, characters, conflict, and resolution with students. Post the following definitions for students on chart paper or the board:

> *setting:* the location of the story in time and place
>
> *characters*: the people, animals, or other creatures in the story
>
> *conflict*: the struggle between two people or things in the story
>
> *resolution*: the solution to the conflict

❸ Have students put their names at the top of a piece of lined paper. Explain that in this activity, there will be several writing periods of about three minutes each. After each writing period, students will pass their papers to the person seated behind them. The person in the back will walk his or her paper to the person at the front of the row.

Story Elements

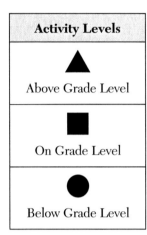

4 Tell students that they will begin by introducing the setting of the story. Encourage them to be creative. Set the timer for three minutes and have students write.

5 After three minutes, have students pass their papers. Instruct them to read the story on the new paper. Explain that they will be adding on to this story. This time, they will introduce one to three main characters. The characters should fit the setting they were given. Set the timer and allow students to write.

6 After three minutes, have students pass their papers again. Instruct them to read the story on the new paper. This time, they will introduce a problem for the main character or characters. Set the timer and allow students to write.

7 Continue to have students pass their papers after three minutes and read the story again. Instruct them to write about either the characters trying to solve the problem but failing to do so, or the characters successfully solving the conflict (the resolution). Have students wrap up the story with a lesson or a funny line that ties it all together.

8 Have students return the papers to the original authors.

9 Students will work with story elements in a variety of different ways. Distribute the *Story Elements Choices Board* activity sheet (page 48) to students and assign them a shape according to their readiness levels. Or, distribute the leveled *Story Elements Choices Cards* activity sheets (pages 49–51) to students based on their readiness levels. Review the activity options with students and explain that they will need to complete two activities that correspond to their assigned shapes.

10 If students finish early, they may complete the Anchor Activity.

Assessment

Assess student understanding of story elements by evaluating the work they completed from their choices boards. Prepare to work with small groups to reinforce or reteach any confusing concepts.

Activity Levels
▲
Above Grade Level
■
On Grade Level
●
Below Grade Level

Anchor Activity

Have students write a story that brings the story elements together in a clever way. Ahead of time, write several settings, character types, and conflict ideas on three different colored slips of paper. Each type of story element should be on a different color of paper. Put each type of story element in a separate bag. Allow students to draw a slip from each bag and use those elements in their story.

Name _____

Story Elements Choices Board

Directions: Circle two activities to complete from the choices board below. Be sure to match the shape(s) assigned to you by your teacher.

Find a painting that you really like. Study the setting and characters. Imagine a conflict and a resolution in the painting. Write a story about it using all of the story elements. ▲	Write a story on sentence strips. Use all of the story elements. Mix up the order of the story and challenge a friend to put the story in order. ●	Choose a picture book that you enjoy. Write a sequel to that book. Be sure to think of a new conflict and resolution for the characters. ■
Write a comic strip. Use all of the story elements. Illustrate and color your final product. It should have five or six frames. ●	Research an insect. Think about its habitat and predators. Then, write a story about a day in the life of your bug. Include all of the story elements. Make sure that your story is based on facts. ■	Write a short skit using all of the story elements. Include a description of the setting, and make sure that the dialogue includes a conflict and resolution. Invite some friends to perform the skit with you for the class. ▲
Pick a favorite book character. Imagine you are interviewing the character from the story. Write the questions that you would ask and the answers that you imagine the character would give. ■	Create a slide show presentation that explains each story element and gives an example of each. The presentation should be at least four slides long. ▲	Pick a chapter book you have recently read. On an index card, explain the setting, main characters, conflict, and resolution for this book. ●
Pick a fairy tale that you enjoy. Pretend that the ending did not work out correctly and there was no resolution. Retell the fairy tale and explain how this affects the story. ▲	Read two versions of the same fairy tale. Which one do you like best? Write a paragraph telling why you like it better. ●	Pick a fairy tale that you enjoy. Change the setting to a modern-day place and rewrite it. Make adjustments to the fairy tale, as needed. ■

Name _____

Story Elements Choices Cards

Directions: Choose activities from the cards below.

Pick a fairy tale that you enjoy. Pretend that the ending did not work out correctly and there was no resolution. Retell the fairy tale and explain how this affects the story.

Write a short skit using all of the story elements. Include a description of the setting, and make sure that the dialogue includes a conflict and resolution. Invite some friends to perform the skit with you for the class.

Create a slide show presentation that explains each story element and gives an example of each. The presentation should be at least four slides long.

Find a painting that you really like. Study the setting and characters. Imagine a conflict and a resolution in the painting. Write a story about it using all of the story elements.

Story Elements Choices Cards

Directions: Choose activities from the cards below.

Research an insect. Think about its habitat and predators. Then, write a story about a day in the life of your bug. Include all of the story elements. Make sure that your story is based on facts.

Choose a picture book that you enjoy. Write a sequel to that book. Be sure to think of a new conflict and resolution for the characters.

Pick a favorite book character. Imagine you are interviewing the character from the story. Write the questions that you would ask and the answers that you imagine the character would give.

Pick a fairy tale you enjoy. Change the setting to a modern-day place and rewrite it. Make adjustments to the fairy tale, as needed.

Name _____

Story Elements Choices Cards

Directions: Choose activities from the cards below.

Read two versions of the same fairy tale. Which one do you like best? Write a paragraph telling why you like it better.	Pick a chapter book you have recently read. On an index card, explain the setting, main characters, conflict, and resolution for this book.
Write a comic strip. Use all of the story elements. Illustrate and color your final product. It should have five or six frames.	Write a story on sentence strips. Use all of the story elements. Mix up the order of the story and challenge a friend to put the story in order.

Haiku Poetry

Differentiation Strategy

 Multiple Intelligences

Standards

- Students will write narrative accounts, such as poems and stories.

- TESOL: Students will use the appropriate language variety, register, and genre according to audience, purpose, and setting.

Materials

- lesson resources (pages 54–57)

- books of poetry (See page 167.)

- examples of haiku poems (See page 167.)

- Internet

- art supplies

Procedures

1 Begin by reading several haiku poems aloud to the class. Ask students to describe the features of the poems they heard. They might say that the poems are short. They also might notice that they are not written in complete sentences and are missing some words.

2 Explain that these poems are examples of *haiku* poetry. The haiku is a form of poetry that came from Japan. A haiku has three lines. The first line has five syllables. The second line has seven syllables. The third line has five syllables. The goal of a haiku is to paint a picture with words. Most traditional Japanese poems are about nature and, more specifically, the seasons. These poems are simple and elegant. Students will be amazed by how poetic their ideas sound when written in haiku form.

3 Brainstorm a list of nature topics as a class. Some suggestions include lightning, waves, weeping-willow trees, frogs, mosquitoes, and tulips. Next, conduct a shared-writing activity in which the class writes one haiku together on the board.

4 Have students practice writing two or three haiku poems independently. Allow time for students to share their poems with the class.

★ **English Language Support**—Spend some time practicing the skill of syllable counting with English language learners and other struggling students. Pronounce words together and clap the beats of the syllables.

5 Tell students that they will get a chance to play with haiku poetry with many unique activities. Briefly explain the concept of multiple intelligences if your students are unfamiliar with this idea. Tell students that people have different strengths and learn in a variety of ways. Share examples of gifted athletes, artists, writers, actors, and musicians. Explain that students have their own strengths and that these activities will help them discover and identify their preferred learning styles.

Haiku Poetry

6 Display the *Making Sense of Multiple Intelligences* activity sheet (page 54). Read aloud the list of multiple intelligences, and have students think-pair-share about their strengths and preferred learning styles.

7 Distribute the *Haiku Poetry and Multiple Intelligences* activity sheets (pages 55–56) to students. Explain to students that they will choose several activities to complete. Because of their varied learning styles, students will find some activities easier than others. Their opinions on how interesting or challenging an activity is will vary.

8 If students finish early, they may complete the Anchor Activity.

Assessment

Use the *Haiku Poetry Rubric* (page 57) to evaluate students' work. You will want to use one rubric for each project students complete; for example, if you assign four projects, you will use four rubrics for each student.

Anchor Activity

Have students come up with another haiku project that fits their learning style. Help students choose their strongest multiple intelligence to use in designing a project. Have them write guidelines for the project. Then, ask them to follow their own guidelines to complete the project.

Name _____

Making Sense of Multiple Intelligences

Directions: Read through the definitions of the multiple intelligences below. Think about which ones describe your strengths the best.

 Verbal/Linguistic Intelligence—Word Smart

This is the ability to read, write, and communicate with words.

 Logical/Mathematical Intelligence—Number Smart

This is the ability to look for patterns, reason, and think in a logical manner.

 Visual/Spatial Intelligence—Picture Smart

This is the ability to think in pictures and visualize outcomes.

 Musical/Rhythmic Intelligence—Music Smart

This is the ability to make and compose music, sing, and use rhythm to learn.

 Bodily/Kinesthetic Intelligence—Body Smart

This is the ability to think in body movements and to use the body to solve problems.

 Interpersonal Intelligence—People Smart

This is the ability to communicate and empathize with other people.

 Intrapersonal Intelligence—Self Smart

This is the ability to draw upon your own feelings as a guide for decisions and behavior.

 Naturalist Intelligence—Nature Smart

This is the ability to make distinctions in nature and the environment.

 Existential—Deep-Question Smart

This is the ability to pose thoughtful questions about the meaning of life and to understand the "big picture."

Haiku Poetry and Multiple Intelligences

A *haiku* is a Japanese poem that uses a few carefully chosen images. A haiku has three lines. The first line has five syllables. The second line has seven syllables. The third line has five syllables. See the example below.

Mama's garden gate
bright pink flowers shout the news
finally it's spring!

Directions: Complete _____ of the haiku activities below. Read the directions for each project carefully. **Projects are due:_____.**

 ## Verbal/Linguistic

One way to bring your haiku to life is to use personification. Personification is when you make an object (like a tree or a chair) do what people do. In the example above, the flowers are personified by shouting. Practice personifying a few objects. Then, choose your favorite image. Use it in at least two haiku poems.

 ## Visual/Spatial

Choose one of the haiku poems you have written. Illustrate it with a creative collage. Choose surprising objects and put them together in a unique way.

 ## Bodily/Kinesthetic

Choose your favorite haiku to recite to the class. Memorize the title, the author's name, and the poem itself. Practice performing it with vocal expression and hand gestures. Perform for the class when you are ready.

 ## Interpersonal

Research the life and work of a famous haiku poet. On a day chosen by your teacher, come to school dressed as that person. Introduce the poet to your classmates and tell a little about his or her life and work. Be prepared to read or recite some of your poet's poems.

Name _____

Haiku Poetry and Multiple Intelligences (cont.)

 Intrapersonal

Close your eyes and picture a place that makes you feel safe and happy. This might be your room at home or a spot under a favorite tree in the park. It could be cuddling on the couch with your dog or swimming underwater. When you clearly see the image, make a list of words describing what you see and feel. Then, turn your list into a haiku.

+ −
× ÷ **Logical/Mathematical**

The haiku follows a five-seven-five syllable pattern. Play with other possible word and syllable patterns. Choose a topic that has meaning to you and write two poems about it. One should follow the haiku format, and the other should follow your original pattern. Which poem do you like best?

 Musical/Rhythmic

Choose your three favorite haiku poems. These could be written by you or by a famous poet. Read the poems many times. As you read, think about the way the words make you feel. Then, choose a song that makes you feel the same way. Put together a presentation of the three poems and three songs. Be prepared to explain your choices.

 Naturalist

Get outdoors and enjoy nature. Take a hike or just sit and enjoy the view. Bring along your paper and pencil. When you see something that inspires you, stop and write. You could start by making a list of descriptive words and images, or you could write a complete haiku. In the end, you will hand in three nature haiku poems.

 Existential

Research the history of haiku poetry. What place does this art form have in Japanese culture? Write a short paper that will help your classmates understand the importance of haiku poems.

Name _____

Haiku Poetry Rubric

Reading the Rubric: Your project has been graded on five criteria. You earned a score from 1 to 5 for each item. Your project is worth a total of 25 points.

Criteria	Poor	Needs Work	Fair	Strong	Excellent
You followed project guidelines.	1	2	3	4	5
You used the five-seven-five syllable pattern.	1	2	3	4	5
You painted a picture with words.	1	2	3	4	5
Your work is creative and original.	1	2	3	4	5
It is obvious that you proofread your writing or prepared your presentation.	1	2	3	4	5

Score: _____ /25

Teacher Comments: _____

_____

_____

– –

Name _____

Haiku Poetry Rubric

Reading the Rubric: Your project has been graded on five criteria. You earned a score from 1 to 5 for each item. Your project is worth a total of 25 points.

Criteria	Poor	Needs Work	Fair	Strong	Excellent
You followed project guidelines.	1	2	3	4	5
You used the five-seven-five syllable pattern.	1	2	3	4	5
You painted a picture with words.	1	2	3	4	5
Your work is creative and original.	1	2	3	4	5
It is obvious that you proofread your writing or prepared your presentation.	1	2	3	4	5

Score: _____ /25

Teacher Comments: _____

_____

_____

Number Sense

Differentiation Strategy

Choices Board

Standards

- Students will understand the basic meaning of place value.
- TESOL: Students will use English to interact in the classroom.

Materials

- lesson resources (pages 60–63)
- sample restaurant menus
- Internet
- school supply list

Procedures

1. Choose a secret number within a specific range, such as 1 to 1,000 or 250 to 750. Tell students the range. Have volunteers take turns guessing the number. After each guess, give students a clue about the secret number. For example, if the secret number is 639, you might give the clue that the digit in the hundreds place is greater than five.

2. Place students with partners who are at the same readiness levels. Have them take turns playing the secret number game for a few minutes. Meet with students working below grade level in a small group to support students as they take turns playing this game.

3. Some students may benefit from a review of the basics of place value, rounding, and computation with money. You could pull small groups of students to review each concept while the rest of the class begins work on their activities. For students spending much of the class time in reviews, you might consider reducing the number of activities they are required to complete or providing extra work time. Concepts for review may include the following:

- place value through the hundred thousands
- rounding six-digit numbers to each place
- adding numbers through 100,000
- subtracting numbers through 100,000

 © *Shell Education*

Number Sense

❹ Distribute copies of the *Number Sense Choices Board* (page 60) to students and assign students a shape based on their readiness levels. Have above-grade-level students choose two triangle activities to complete, one independently and one with a friend. Have on-grade-level students choose one square activity to complete independently and one triangle activity to complete with a friend. Have below-grade-level students choose one circle activity to complete independently and one square activity to complete with a friend. Another option is to distribute the leveled *Number Sense Choices Cards* activity sheets (pages 61–63) to students based on readiness levels. This will allow them to choose activities at their levels only.

★ **English Language Support**—Read the choices aloud to English language learners, as needed. Provide definitions and examples of key vocabulary terms.

❺ If students finish early, they may complete the Anchor Activity.

Activity Levels
▲
Above Grade Level
■
On Grade Level
●
Below Grade Level

Assessment

Monitor students as they work to make sure that they are working on problems that appropriately challenge them. Make adjustments as needed and reassign problems that offer just the right amount of challenge.

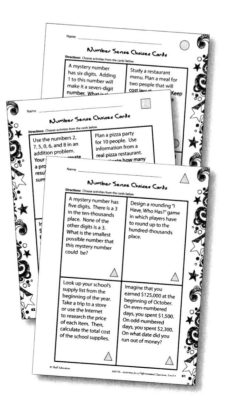

Anchor Activity

Have students create their own three-by-three choices board. Instruct them to fill the board with number sense problems, some that are easy, some challenging, and others very difficult.

Name _____

Number Sense Choices Board

Directions: Circle two activities to complete from the choice board below. Be sure to match the shape(s) assigned to you by your teacher.

I will choose _____ _____ activity to complete by myself
            (number)   (shape)

and _____ _____ activity to complete with a friend.
     (number)   (shape)

Use the numbers 2, 7, 5, 0, 6, and 8 in an addition problem. Your goal is to create a problem that will result in the largest sum possible. ▢	A mystery number has five digits. There is a 3 in the ten-thousands place. None of the other digits is a 3. What is the smallest possible number that this mystery number could be? △	A mystery number has six digits. Adding 1 to this number will make it a seven-digit number. What is the mystery number? ◯
Study a restaurant menu. Plan a meal for two people that will cost less than $20. Keep track of your choices and calculations. ◯	Plan a pizza party for 10 people. Use information from a real pizza restaurant. Investigate how many pizzas you will need to buy in order to give each person three slices. How much will it cost for the pizzas and delivery? ▢	Look up your school's supply list from the beginning of the year. Take a trip to a store or use the Internet to research the price of each item. Then, calculate the total cost of the school supplies. △
Imagine that you earned $125,000 at the beginning of October. On even-numbered days, you spent $1,500. On odd-numbered days, you spent $2,300. On what date did you run out of money? △	Imagine that you earned $10,000 at the beginning of November. On even-numbered days, you spent $100. On odd-numbered days you spent $200. On what date did you run out of money? ◯	Imagine that you earned $100,000 at the beginning of December. On even-numbered days, you spent $1,000. On odd-numbered days, you spent $1,500. On what date did you run out of money? ▢
Design a rounding card game in which players have to round numbers up to the thousands place. ◯	Design a rounding dice game in which players have to round numbers up to the ten-thousands place. ▢	Design a rounding "I Have, Who Has?" game in which players have to round up to the hundred-thousands place △

© Shell Education

Name _____

Number Sense Choices Cards

Directions: Choose activities from the cards below.

A mystery number has five digits. There is a 3 in the ten-thousands place. None of the other digits is a 3. What is the smallest possible number that this mystery number could be?

Design a rounding "I Have, Who Has?" game in which players have to round up to the hundred-thousands place.

Look up your school's supply list from the beginning of the year. Take a trip to a store or use the Internet to research the price of each item. Then, calculate the total cost of the school supplies.

Imagine that you earned $125,000 at the beginning of October. On even-numbered days, you spent $1,500. On odd-numbered days, you spent $2,300. On what date did you run out of money?

Name _____

Number Sense Choices Cards

Directions: Choose activities from the cards below.

Use the numbers 2, 7, 5, 0, 6, and 8 in an addition problem. Your goal is to create a problem that will result in the largest sum possible.	Plan a pizza party for 10 people. Use information from a real pizza restaurant. Investigate how many pizzas you will need to buy in order to give each person three slices. How much will it cost for the pizzas and delivery?
Imagine you earned $100,000 at the beginning of December. On even-numbered days, you spent $1,000. On odd-numbered days, you spent $1,500. On what date did you run out of money?	Design a rounding dice game in which players have to round numbers up to the ten-thousands place.

Number Sense Choices Cards

Directions: Choose activities from the cards below.

A mystery number has six digits. Adding 1 to this number will make it a seven-digit number. What is the mystery number?

Study a restaurant menu. Plan a meal for two people that will cost less than $20. Keep track of your choices and calculations.

Imagine that you earned $10,000 at the beginning of November. On even-numbered days, you spent $100. On odd-numbered days you spent $200. On what date did you run out of money?

Design a rounding card game in which players round numbers up to the thousands place.

Decimals

Differentiation Strategy

 Multiple Intelligences

Standards

- Students will add and subtract decimals.

- TESOL: Students will use English to interact in the classroom.

Materials

- lesson resources (pages 66–69)

- scissors

- plastic storage bags

- coins

- bowl

- game pieces

- meter sticks, one per student pair

- centimeter cubes and rods

- stopwatch

- Internet

- audio recorder

- thermometer

- play money

- art supplies

Procedures

Preparation Note: Make copies of the *Decimal Cards* (page 66). Each pair of students will need a set of cards. Cut the cards out and store them in plastic bags.

❶ Review decimals with your students. Explain that a decimal is another way to represent a fraction, or part of a whole number. Review how decimals relate to money, pointing out that coins are a fraction of a whole dollar, and are written as decimals. Strengthen this connection by placing some coins in a bowl. Have volunteers draw a few coins out of the bowl. Then, on the board, do several sample addition and subtraction problems using the combinations of coins taken from the bowl. Emphasize the importance of recognizing decimal place value and lining up the decimal points in addition and subtraction problems.

❷ Allow students to choose a partner for a class game called *Race to a Meter*.

★ **English Language Support**—Pair these students with partners who are fluent in English. This will provide support as students read the game directions. It will also give English language learners a chance to practice their language skills in casual conversation.

❸ Distribute two game pieces, one meter stick, centimeter cubes and rods, and one set of *Decimal Cards* (page 66) to each pair of students.

❹ Students should place the meter stick on the floor between them and their game pieces at the zero mark. One player will move his or her game piece along the left side of the meter stick and the other player will move along the right side.

Decimals

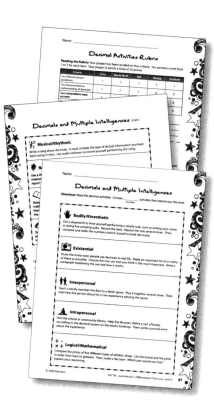

⑤ Students will take turns drawing *Decimal Cards* from the deck. The decimals on the cards represent a part of one whole meter. (A decimal of 0.1 would be equivalent to 10 centimeters, and 0.01 would be equivalent to one centimeter.)

⑥ Each card has an addition sign or a subtraction sign with a decimal. Adding decimals will make players' game pieces move forward along the meter stick, and subtracting decimals will make players' game pieces move backward.

⑦ Explain that the centimeter cubes and rods will help players measure each move their game piece makes during the game. Show the students how the centimeter cubes exactly match the marks on the meter stick and how the rods match groups of 10. Give the students time to explore this concept.

⑧ The first player to reach the opposite end of the stick wins. Pairs who finish early can switch partners, shuffle the cards, and play again.

⑨ Distribute the *Decimals and Multiple Intelligences* activity sheets (pages 67–68) to students. Determine the number of activities that students should complete and a due date for the projects. Review the options as a class and encourage students to complete the activities that they find most appealing based on their learning styles.

⑩ If students finish early, they may complete the Anchor Activity.

Assessment

Use the *Decimal Activities Rubric* (page 69) to evaluate students' work. Use one rubric for each project that a student completes.

Anchor Activity

Have students create a new game in which players work with decimal numbers. Suggest that a good starting point is to think about the games that they enjoy playing. They can model their decimal games on those games.

Name _____

Decimal Cards

Directions: Carefully cut out the Decimal Cards for the game. Mark the back of the card in some distinct way so that lost cards can be returned to your set. Store the cards in a plastic storage bag or envelope.

+ 0.52	+ 0.42	+ 0.02	+ 0.10
− 0.7	+ 0.23	− 0.05	− 0.01
+ 0.21	− 0.63	+ 0.31	+ 0.50
+ 0.07	+ 0.06	+ 0.0	+ 0.55
+ 0.33	+ 0.21	+ 0.09	+ 0.25
− 0.45	+ 0.29	− 0.08	− 0.04
+ 0.38	− 0.20	+ 0.44	+ 0.01
+ 0.03	+ 0.4	− 0.0	− 0.4

© *Shell Education*

Name _____

Decimals and Multiple Intelligences

Directions: Read the decimal activities. Choose _____ activities that interest you the most.
(number)

 Bodily/Kinesthetic

Use a stopwatch to time yourself performing a simple task, such as writing your name or doing five jumping jacks. Record the data. Repeat the task several times. Then, compare and order the numbers (which should include decimals).

 Existential

Study the many ways people use decimals in real life. Make an organized list of as many of these as possible. Choose the one use that you think is the most important. Write a paragraph explaining the use and how it works.

 Interpersonal

Teach a family member the *Race to a Meter* game. Play it together several times. Then interview the person about his or her experience playing the game.

 Intrapersonal

Visit the school or community library. Help the librarian shelve a cart of books according to the decimal system on the books' bindings. Then, write a journal entry about the experience.

+ –
× ÷ Logical/Mathematical

Compare the prices of five different types of athletic shoes. List the brand and the price in order from least to greatest. Then, make a decision. Which pair would you buy? Explain your reasoning.

Decimals and Multiple Intelligences *(cont.)*

Musical/Rhythmic

Write a song about decimals. It must include the type of factual information you have been using in class. Use audio software to record yourself performing the song.

Naturalist

Use a thermometer to track the temperature every day for two weeks. Your measurements should include decimal numbers. Compare the measurements. Then, report your findings on a chart or graph.

Verbal/Linguistic

Design a game that uses play money. The game should involve buying items and making change. Write the directions for the game in clear, simple terms. Observe as friends try to follow the directions and play the game. Use their feedback to improve the directions, as needed.

Visual/Spatial

Design a poster that shows how to add and subtract decimals. Include sample problems on the poster. Add artwork and lettering to make your poster visually appealing.

My Action Plan

I plan to complete the following project or projects:

_____

_____

_____

I will need to take these steps to complete my work:

_____

_____

_____

Projects are due: _____

Name _____

Decimal Activities Rubric

Reading the Rubric: Your project has been graded on four criteria. You earned a score from 1 to 5 for each item. Your project is worth a total of 20 points.

Criteria	Poor	Needs Work	Fair	Strong	Excellent
You followed project guidelines.	1	2	3	4	5
You demonstrated an understanding of decimals.	1	2	3	4	5
Your computations were accurate.	1	2	3	4	5
Your work is neat, careful, and shows effort.	1	2	3	4	5

Score _____ /20

Teacher Comments: _____

_____

_____

— —

Name _____

Decimal Activities Rubric

Reading the Rubric: Your project has been graded on four criteria. You earned a score from 1 to 5 for each item. Your project is worth a total of 20 points.

Criteria	Poor	Needs Work	Fair	Strong	Excellent
You followed project guidelines.	1	2	3	4	5
You demonstrated an understanding of decimals.	1	2	3	4	5
Your computations were accurate.	1	2	3	4	5
Your work is neat, careful, and shows effort.	1	2	3	4	5

Score _____ /20

Teacher Comments: _____

_____

_____

Measuring and Graphing

Differentiation Strategy

 Tiered Graphic Organizers

Standards

• Students will organize and display data in simple bar graphs.

• TESOL: Students will use appropriate learning strategies to construct and apply academic knowledge.

Materials

• lesson resources (pages 72–75)

• masking tape

• chalk

• measuring tapes or yardsticks

• adding-machine paper

Procedures

1 Assess what students know about converting measurements by having them complete the *Converting Measurements Assessment* activity sheet (page 72).

2 Ask a volunteer to perform a standing long jump as you explain the feat. The jumper begins with his or her toes touching the starting line, then squats and springs forward as far as possible. The jumper must freeze upon landing.

3 Invite another volunteer to show the class how to measure the jumper's distance. The volunteer taking the measurement will make a chalk mark on the ground at the heel of the jumper's shoe. The volunteers can work together to measure the distance from the starting line to the chalk mark. Record the distance on the board.

4 Explain that all students will have a chance to practice the standing long jump for a math activity. Based on the results of the assessment in step 1, place students in homogeneous groups of four or five. Explain that each group will use masking tape, chalk, and measuring tapes or yardsticks to measure and record the distance of group members' jumps. Each student may jump twice, and one group member can record the distance (in inches) of the farthest jump.

5 After students have measured and recorded their jumps, have them create paper representations of their jumps using adding-machine paper. On the adding-machine paper, have students measure, in inches, the distance that they jumped. Then, they will cut the paper to the length of their jumps. Have them record their names and distances clearly on the bottom of the strips.

Measuring and Graphing

6 Choose a wall where you can hang students' jump strips vertically. The strips should be lined up along the floor and spaced about one centimeter apart. This will create a giant bar graph of students' jump data.

7 On the wall graph, label the x-axis and the y-axis. Explain to students that the x-axis is the horizontal axis. In this case, it is the line where the wall meets the floor. It could be titled *Jumpers*. The y-axis is the vertical axis. This axis should be labeled *Distance Jumped (in inches)*. Invite students to make observations about the data and discuss their ideas.

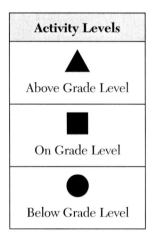

Activity Levels
▲ Above Grade Level
■ On Grade Level
● Below Grade Level

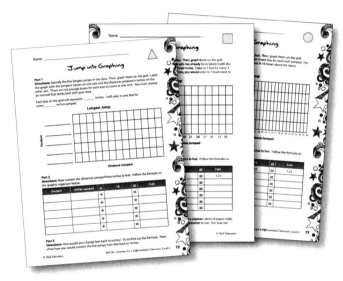

8 Ask students to return to their groups for more graphing practice. Distribute the *Jump into Graphing* activity sheets (pages 73–75) to students based on their readiness levels. Point out that the bar graphs on the activity sheets are oriented horizontally.

★ **English Language Support**—Read the directions aloud to these students. Review the locations of the x-axis and y-axis on the graph.

9 If students finish early, they may complete the Anchor Activity.

Assessment

Use the *Converting Measurements Assessment* activity sheet (page 72) as both a pre- and post-test to monitor students' progress and understanding.

Anchor Activity

Have students design an activity that will provide data, similar to the standing long-jump activity. Then, ask students to research the different types of graphs. They should choose the best type of graph for their data and create it. To design the graph, they should use the best tools available to them, from paper and coloring supplies to computer software.

Name _____

Converting Measurements Assessment

> There are 12 inches in a foot. One foot equals 12 inches.

Part 1

Directions: Use the formula to convert inches to feet.

$$\_\_\_\_\_ \text{ inches} \div 12 = \_\_\_\_\_ \text{ feet}$$

1. 36 in. = _____ ft.
2. 12 in. = _____ ft.
3. 48 in. = _____ ft.
4. 24 in. = _____ ft.
5. 60 in. = _____ ft.

6. 72 in. = _____ ft.
7. 96 in. = _____ ft.
8. _____ in. = 7 ft.
9. _____ in. = 4 ft.
10. _____ in. = 5 ft.

Part 2

Directions: Use the formula to convert feet to inches.

$$\_\_\_ \text{ feet} \times 12 = \_\_\_ \text{ inches}$$

1. 4 ft. = _____ in.
2. 7 ft. = _____ in.
3. 2 ft. = _____ in.
4. 9 ft. = _____ in.
5. 10 ft. = _____ in.

6. 5 ft. = _____ in.
7. 1 ft. = _____ in.
8. _____ ft. = 36 in.
9. _____ ft. = 72 in.
10. _____ ft. = 48 in.

Part 3

Directions: In some cases, it would make more sense to measure in inches. In other cases, measuring in feet makes more sense.

1. List three things that you would measure in inches.

    • _____

    • _____

    • _____

2. List three things that you would measure in feet.

    • _____

    • _____

    • _____

© *Shell Education*

Name _____

Jump into Graphing

Part 1

Directions: Identify the five longest jumps in the class. Then, graph them on the grid. Label the graph with the jumpers' names on one axis and the distances jumped in inches on the other axis. There are not enough boxes for each box to count as one inch. You must choose an interval that works best with your data.

Each box on the grid will represent _____ inches. I will color one box for every _____ inches jumped.

Longest Jump

Student

Distance Jumped

Part 2

Directions: Now convert the distances jumped from inches to feet. Follow the formula on the graphic organizer below.

Student	Inches Jumped	÷	12	=	Feet
		÷		=	
		÷		=	
		÷		=	
		÷		=	
		÷		=	

Part 3

Directions: How would you change feet back to inches? Try to find out the formula. Then, show how you would convert the five jumps from feet back to inches.

Name _____

Jump into Graphing

Part 1

Directions: Identify the five longest jumps in the class. Then, graph them on the grid. Write the five jumpers' names along the *y*-axis. The *x*-axis has already been labeled with the number of inches. Each box on the grid represents three inches. Color 1 box for every 3 inches jumped. For example, if Logan jumped 15 inches, you would color 5 boxes next to his name.

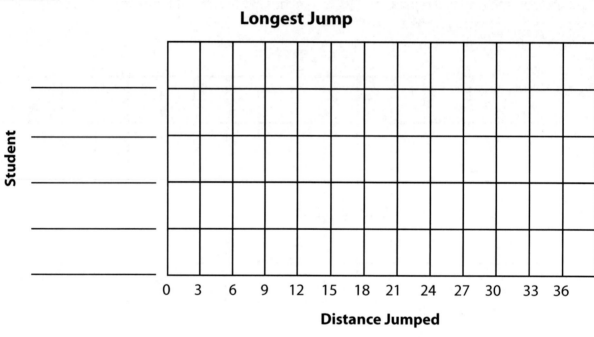

Longest Jump

Student

Distance Jumped

Part 2

Directions: Now convert the distances jumped from inches to feet. Follow the formula on the graphic organizer below.

Student	Inches Jumped	÷	12	=	Feet
Logan	15	÷	12	=	1.25
		÷		=	
		÷		=	
		÷		=	
		÷		=	
		÷		=	
		÷		=	

Part 3

Directions: How would you change feet back to inches? On a separate sheet of paper, make a graphic organizer. Try some problems and decide which operation to use. You may use a calculator.

Name _____

Jump into Graphing

Part 1

Directions: Identify the five longest jumps in the class. Then, graph them on the grid. Write the five jumpers' names along the *y*-axis. Color one box for each inch jumped. For example, if Logan jumped 15 inches, you would color 15 boxes above his name.

Part 2

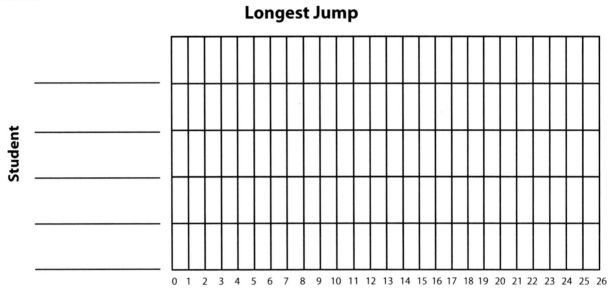

Longest Jump

Student

_____

_____

_____

_____

_____

0 1 2 3 4 5 6 7 8 9 10 11 12 13 14 15 16 17 18 19 20 21 22 23 24 25 26

Distance Jumped

Directions: Now change the distances jumped from inches to feet. Follow the formula on the graphic organizer below.

Student	Inches Jumped	÷	12	=	Feet
Logan	15	÷	12	=	1.25
		÷		=	
		÷		=	
		÷		=	
		÷		=	
		÷		=	

Fractions

Differentiation Strategy

 Leveled Questions

Standards

- Students will understand the concepts related to fractions and decimals.

- TESOL: Students will use appropriate learning strategies to construct and apply academic knowledge.

Materials

- lesson resources (pages 78–81)

- one full-size chocolate bar with 12 segments, such as a Hershey's® bar

- miniature chocolate bars

Procedures

1 Walk around the classroom showing students a chocolate bar. Ask them if all halves are the same. Most students will answer yes to this question because they are focused on the chocolate.

2 Break the chocolate bar in half. Ask one student if he or she would like half. Do not say specifically half of what. Then, set down the large chocolate bar and take out a miniature chocolate bar. Break the miniature bar in half and give that to the student. Watch the students' reactions and act surprised. Say, *"What's wrong? I gave half. You said all halves are the same."* Allow students to discuss this concept and revise their answer. Lead them to the idea that the sizes of halves depend on the sizes of the wholes. Now is a great time to give each student a miniature chocolate bar, if you choose.

3 Show students that there are a total of 12 segments in the large chocolate bar. Explain that in this case, there are 12 parts in one whole. On the board, write $\frac{12}{12}$ = 1 whole.

4 Break the bar into 12 segments and stack them on top of each other. Ask students if $\frac{12}{12}$ or 1 whole is still an accurate description of the chocolate bar. Take away one segment and explain that this small amount could be described as $\frac{1}{12}$ of the whole chocolate bar. On the board, draw one rectangle and write $\frac{1}{12}$. Ask a volunteer to come to the board to sketch the remaining pieces of chocolate and write a fraction that describes the amount ($\frac{11}{12}$). Continue this activity by having students sketch and write fractions on the board to describe the different amounts of chocolate.

5 Ask students to think of another name for $\frac{6}{12}$. Show the students two equal stacks of chocolate segments. Each has six pieces. That means one stack equals half of the whole bar. In this case, $\frac{6}{12} = \frac{1}{2}$. Discuss this important fraction.

6 Now ask students to think about how the fractions would change if the chocolate bar had 16 total segments. Sketch a 16-segment bar and a 12-segment bar on the board to help students see the difference. Ask students to write fractions that describe parts of the 16-piece bar.

  © *Shell Education*

Fractions

7 Ask volunteers to come to the board to shade half of the segments of the 16-segment bar and half of the pieces of the 12-segment bar. For the smaller bar, $\frac{6}{12}$ is half. For the larger bar, $\frac{8}{16}$ would be half. Invite students to explain the pattern they see in these two examples. Point out that the top number (numerator) is half of the bottom number (denominator). Write other examples of half to show students the pattern.

8 Tell students that they will now answer questions based on the class activity. Distribute the *Fractions in Action* activity sheets (pages 78–80) to students based on their readiness levels. Bring the below-grade-level students together to work with you in a group.

★ **English Language Support**—Pair these students with English-proficient students. Encourage the English-proficient students to review and explain vocabulary, as needed.

9 As an extension, distribute copies of the *Fractions All Around Us* activity sheet (pages 81). Place students in heterogeneous small groups for this activity. Students will use the chocolate bar lesson as inspiration for writing a fractions lesson plan of their own. If possible, give students opportunities to teach their lessons to other fourth graders.

10 If students finish early, they may complete the Anchor Activity.

Assessment

As students are working on their assignments, walk around the class and be available to help students. Grade students' work to assess if they understand the concepts taught in this lesson.

Activity Levels

Activity Levels
▲
Above Grade Level
■
On Grade Level
●
Below Grade Level

Anchor Activity

Have students use Cuisenaire® Rods to model fractional representations. Ask them to make a key that describes each rod as a fraction. First, have students use the 10-centimeter orange rod as the unit or the whole. What fractional value would be assigned to the rest of the rods? Next, have them assume that the blue rod equals one whole. Ask them to assign fractional values to the light green and white rods.

Name _____

Fractions in Action

Directions: Answer the questions about fractions.

1. Draw three different pictures divided into different numbers of parts to show one whole. Write the fraction that describes each picture.

 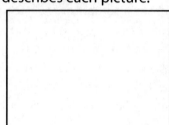 

2. Explain how the fractions in problem 1 are all equal to one whole.

_____

_____

_____

3. Draw three different pictures to show $\frac{1}{2}$. Write the fraction that describes each picture.

4. Draw pictures to show each fraction. Can any of the fractions be described using different numbers? If so, write the new fraction next to the original.

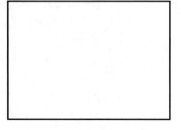 

$\frac{1}{5}$ $\frac{2}{5}$ $\frac{7}{8}$

Name _____

Fractions in Action

Directions: Answer the questions. Think about the class activity as you work.

1. Shade the circles to show one whole. On the line, write the fraction that describes each circle.

    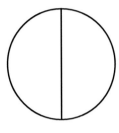   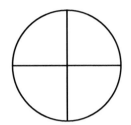   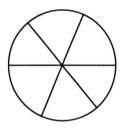

    _____   _____   _____

2. Shade in the rectangles to show $\frac{1}{2}$. On the line, write the fraction that describes each rectangle.

       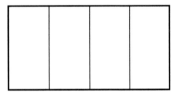   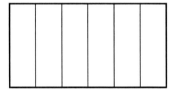

    _____   _____   _____

3. Explain how the fractions $\frac{2}{4}$ and $\frac{5}{10}$ both equal half.

    _____

    _____

    _____

4. Draw pictures to show each fraction.

    $\frac{1}{5}$ $\frac{4}{8}$ $\frac{6}{9}$

Name _____

Fractions in Action

Directions: Answer the questions. Think about the class activity as you work.

1. Shade the circles to show one whole. Complete the fraction to describe each circle.

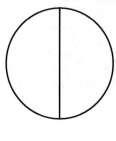 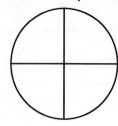 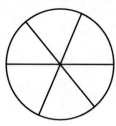

$$\frac{}{2} \qquad\qquad \frac{}{4} \qquad\qquad \frac{}{6}$$

2. Shade in the rectangles to show $\frac{1}{2}$. Complete the fraction to describe each rectangle.

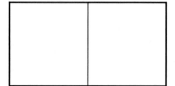  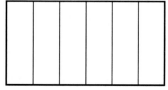

$$\frac{}{2} \qquad\qquad \frac{}{4} \qquad\qquad \frac{}{6}$$

3. The fractions in problem 2 all equal half because _____

_____

_____

4. Shade the rectangles to show each fraction.

    a. $\frac{1}{12}$ 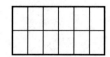   b. $\frac{3}{12}$ 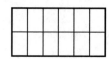   c. $\frac{8}{12}$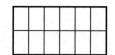

5. Shade the circles to show each fraction.

    $\frac{1}{6}$ 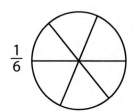 $\frac{2}{6}$ $\frac{5}{6}$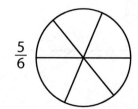

Name _____

Fractions All Around Us

Directions: In class, your teacher used a chocolate bar to teach you about fractions. Can you think of other real-world ways to help other fourth-grade students understand fractions?

1. Make of list of places you find fractions in real life or ways fractions are used in the real world.

   _____
   _____
   _____
   _____
   _____

2. Which of the ideas above could be turned into a creative fraction lesson for other fourth graders?

   _____
   _____
   _____

3. On the back of this page, plan a step-by-step lesson using these steps as a guide.
   Step 1: Grab students' attention.
   Step 2: Explain the concept.
   Step 3: Give students a chance to practice the new concept.
   Step 4: Assess student learning.

4. Explain the main idea that you want students to take away from this lesson.

   _____
   _____
   _____

5. What might make this material difficult for some students?

   _____

6. Think of some ways you can help all students understand the lesson.

   _____
   _____
   _____

7. Make a list of materials that you will need for this lesson.

   _____
   _____
   _____

Perimeter and Area

Differentiation Strategy

 Menu of Options

Standards

- Students will understand relationships between measures, such as area and perimeter.

- TESOL: Students will use English to interact in the classroom.

Materials

- lesson resources (pages 84–87)

- perimeter and area definitions with formulas and illustrations

- index cards

- graph paper

- color tiles

Procedures

1 Ask students to stand up and form a line. Have them slowly walk around the outer edge of the classroom. After students return to their seats, explain that they just walked around the perimeter of the classroom. Post the *perimeter* definition that you prepared ahead of time. Perimeter is the distance around a flat shape. Ask students to picture walking along the walls of the classroom to remind them of the meaning of perimeter.

2 On the board, sketch several rectangles and squares of different sizes. Write numbers that represent the lengths of all four sides of the figures. The numbers should make sense, but measuring your figures is unnecessary. Show students how to add the measures of the four sides to find the perimeter. Invite volunteers to the board to find the perimeter of some of the figures.

3 Distribute one index card to each student. Tell them that they will write their lesson notes on these. The index card will be a handy reference tool for students during independent work. Have students record the formula for the perimeter of a four-sided shape, which is *side + side + side + side = Perimeter*.

4 Have students move their desks or tables to the perimeter of the classroom. Ask them to lie down on the floor with their arms and legs outstretched toward the people around them. As a class, the goal is to cover the floor of the room. Most likely, they will not cover the floor, but students will remember this activity. Explain that this floor space is the area of the classroom.

5 Return to the board. Post the *area* definition that you prepared ahead of time. Area is the amount of space inside a flat shape. Ask students to picture the classroom floor (the space within the walls) to remind them of the meaning of area.

6 Shade the inside of the figures you drew on the board earlier. Show students how to identify the length and width of a figure. Draw horizontal and vertical lines across the figures to indicate the unit length and width. This will create a grid of squares within each shape. Have students count the squares to determine the area of the figure. Then, explain that another way to find the area of a four-sided figure is by multiplying its length and width. Invite volunteers to the board to find the area of the figures. Then, have students write down the area formula of a four-sided shape, which is *Area = length × width*. Be sure to emphasize that area measurements should be given in square units.

Perimeter and Area

6 ★ **English Language Support**—Pull English language learners aside for additional vocabulary work either before or after the lesson. Show them how to run their hands around the outside edges of their desktops or tabletops. Have them repeat the word *perimeter* after you. Ask them to sweep their hands across the tops of their desks. Have them repeat the word *area* after you. Follow the same procedure for the terms *side*, *length*, and *width*. If necessary, students could repeat this exercise using a textbook, a locker, or a cabinet door.

7 Place students in heterogeneous groups. Distribute the *Perimeter and Area Challenge* activity sheet (page 84) to students. Read and complete Part 1 of the activity sheet as a whole class. Show students how to count sides of squares in a figure to find perimeter and to count squares in a figure to find area. Have groups work together to complete the sheet. Ask them to label the perimeter and the area of each shape they draw on the graph paper.

8 When all groups have completed the activity sheet, have students place their papers on top of their desks. Invite students to go on a "gallery walk" to look at their classmates' work. Ask them to compare the work of other groups with their own.

9 Distribute the *Perimeter and Area Menu of Options* activity sheet (page 85). Decide ahead of time the number of points students need to complete and a due date for the projects. Review the project options with the class. Distribute the *Perimeter and Area Project Planning Guide* activity sheet (page 86) to help students prepare for their projects.

10 If students finish early, they may complete the Anchor Activity.

Assessment

Use the *Perimeter and Area Rubric* (page 87) to assess students' work.

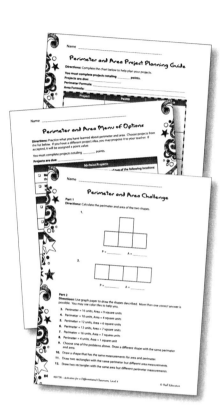

Anchor Activity

Have students measure the sides of 10 square or rectangular objects. Then, ask them to find the perimeter and area of each object. Instruct students to record the object names, side lengths, and calculations on a chart.

Name _____

Perimeter and Area Challenge

Part 1

Directions: Calculate the perimeter and area of the two shapes.

1.

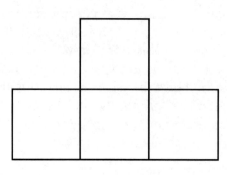

P = _____   A = _____

2.

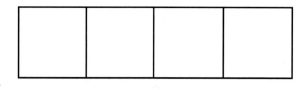

P = _____   A = _____

Part 2

Directions: Use graph paper to draw the shapes described. More than one correct answer is possible. You may use color tiles to help you.

3. Perimeter = 16 units, Area = 9 square units

4. Perimeter = 10 units, Area = 4 square units

5. Perimeter = 12 units, Area = 6 square units

6. Perimeter = 12 units, Area = 7 square units

7. Perimeter = 16 units, Area = 7 square units

8. Perimeter = 4 units, Area = 1 square unit

9. Choose one of the problems above. Draw a different shape with the same perimeter and area.

10. Draw a shape that has the same measurements for area and perimeter.

11. Draw two rectangles with the same perimeter but different area measurements.

12. Draw two rectangles with the same area but different perimeter measurements.

Name _____

Perimeter and Area Menu of Options

Directions: Practice what you have learned about perimeter and area. Choose projects from the list below. If you have a different project idea, you may propose it to your teacher. If accepted, it will be assigned a point value.

You must complete projects totaling _____ points.

Projects are due: _____

50-Point Projects

❑ **Measure the School:** Find the perimeter and area of two of the following locations: the school library, the cafeteria, the playground, or the school gym.

❑ **Measure Your Home:** Find the perimeter and area of at least three rooms in your home. Draw a detailed plan showing the measurements of each room.

30-Point Projects

❑ **Think Like a Mathematician:** Write a mathematical theory about the similarities and differences between perimeter and area. Use mathematical calculations to prove your theory.

❑ **Mathematical Careers:** Make a list of 15 jobs that require workers to use perimeter and area. Explain how each job applies the math concepts.

20-Point Projects

❑ **Drawing Shapes:** If two shapes have the same *area*, must they have the same *perimeter*? Use graph paper to draw shapes that will help you answer this question. Write your answer in complete sentences using your math as proof of your findings.

❑ **Drawing Shapes 2:** If two shapes have the same *perimeter*, can they have the same *area*? Investigate this with graph paper. Then, write your answer in complete sentences using your math as proof of your findings.

10-Point Projects

❑ **A Fence Problem:** Write a word problem about building a fence around a backyard. Include an answer key.

❑ **A Painting Problem:** Write a word problem about painting the walls of a room. Include an answer key.

Name _____

Perimeter and Area Project Planning Guide

Directions: Complete the chart below to help plan your projects.

You must complete projects totaling _____ points.

Projects are due: _____

Perimeter Formula: _____

Area Formula: _____

Project	Points	Steps to Take

Total Points: _____

Name _____

Perimeter and Area Rubric

Directions: Use the chart below to evaluate students' work.

Project	Points Possible	Points Earned
Teacher Comments:	**Total/Grade:**	

— —

Name _____

Perimeter and Area Rubric

Directions: Use the chart below to evaluate students' work.

Project	Points Possible	Points Earned
Teacher Comments:	**Total/Grade:**	

Geometric Transformations

Differentiation Strategy

 Tiered Assignments

Standards

- Students will use motion geometry such as turns, flips, and slides to understand geometric relationships.

- TESOL: Students will use English to interact in the classroom.

Materials

- lesson resources (pages 90–93)

- die-cut letter shapes, one per student

- art supplies

- poster paper

- drawing software *(optional)*

Procedures

1 Begin the lesson by asking students to brainstorm the geometric terms they already know. Make a list of the terms.

2 If students recall the words associated with geometric transformations, include those. If not, add these words: *flips* (reflections), *slides* (translations), and *turns* (rotations). Ask students to guess the definitions of the words. Then, provide them with correct definitions and examples.

- A *reflection* is a transformation that **flips** a figure across a line.

- A *translation* is a transformation that **slides** all points of a figure the same distance in the same direction.

- A *rotation* is a transformation that **turns** a figure around a point.

3 Give each student a piece of drawing paper. Instruct students to fold the paper in half horizontally and vertically to create four equal parts. Then, give each student a die-cut shape.

4 Ask students to write *transformations* in the top-left quadrant of the folded paper. Then, have them write *flip (reflection)* in the top-right quadrant, *slide (translation)* in the bottom right quadrant, and *turn (rotation)* in the bottom-left quadrant.

5 Model each transformation on the board with a die-cut shape. Invite student volunteers to come to the board to try the transformations as you call out the terms.

★ **English Language Support**—Review the vocabulary terms with these students after the lesson. Encourage them to practice moving die-cut shapes as you say the terms.

6 Have students position their die-cut shapes in the top-left quadrants of their papers. Have students trace the shapes in their original positions. Then, have them perform the transformations labeled in each quadrant of their papers. When the die-cut shape is in its transformed position, students should trace it. Encourage students to share their transformations with classmates to check for accuracy and to clarify any misconceptions.

Geometric Transformations

7 For the next activity, place students in homogeneous pairs. Distribute the *Shapes in Motion* activity sheets (pages 90–92) to students based on their readiness levels. Place English language learners in the circle group because of the vocabulary-heavy nature of this lesson. This lesson works well with drawing software. An alternative would be to have students use paper and coloring supplies instead of drawing software to create a scene and label vocabulary words in it.

Activity Levels	
▲
Above Grade Level
■
On Grade Level
●
Below Grade Level

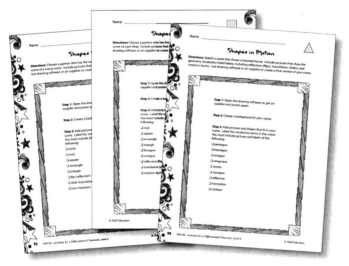

8 When students have finished their work, place them in new heterogeneous groups and allow them to share their presentations, showing their different vocabulary words and scenes.

9 If students finish early, they may complete the Anchor Activity.

Assessment

Assess student learning using the *Shapes in Motion Project Rubric* (page 93).

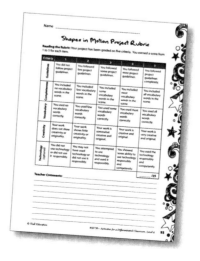

Anchor Activity

Have students write and cut out the letters of their names. Then, have them transform their names by moving the letters in flips, slides, and turns.

Name _____

Shapes in Motion

Directions: Sketch a scene that shows a haunted house. Include pictures that show the geometry vocabulary listed below, including reflections (flips), translations (slides), and rotations (turns). Use drawing software or art supplies to create a final version of your scene.

Step 1: Open the drawing software or get art supplies and poster paper.

Step 2: Create a background for your scene.

Step 3: Add pictures and shapes that fit in your scene. Label the vocabulary terms in the scene. You must include pictures and labels of the following:

❑ pentagon

❑ heptagon

❑ octagon

❑ congruent

❑ similar

❑ nonagon

❑ reflection

❑ translation

❑ rotation

Shapes in Motion

Directions: Choose a partner who has the same activity sheet. Work together to sketch a scene of a pet shop. Include pictures that show the geometry vocabulary words below. Use drawing software or art supplies to create a final version of your scene.

Step 1: Open the drawing software or get art supplies and poster paper.

Step 2: Create a background for your scene.

Step 3: Add pictures and shapes that fit in your scene. Label the vocabulary terms in the scene. You must include pictures and labels of the following:

❑ oval

❑ square

❑ rectangle

❑ triangle

❑ hexagon

❑ octagon

❑ reflection (flip)

❑ translation (slide)

❑ rotation (turn)

Name _____

Shapes in Motion

Directions: Choose a partner who has the same activity sheet. Work together to sketch a scene of a messy room. Include pictures that show the geometry vocabulary words below. Use drawing software or art supplies to create a final version of your scene.

Step 1: Open the drawing software or get art supplies and poster paper.

Step 2: Create a background for your scene.

Step 3: Add pictures and shapes that fit in your scene. Label the vocabulary words in the scene. You must include pictures and labels of the following:

❑ circle

❑ oval

❑ square

❑ rectangle

❑ triangle

❑ flip (reflection)

❑ slide (translation)

❑ turn (rotation)

Name _____

Shapes in Motion Project Rubric

Reading the Rubric: Your project has been graded on five criteria. You earned a score from 1 to 5 for each item.

Criteria	1	2	3	4	5
Guidelines	You did not follow project guidelines.	You followed few project guidelines.	You followed some project guidelines.	You followed most project guidelines.	You followed project guidelines completely.
Completeness	You included no vocabulary words in the scene.	You included few vocabulary words in the scene.	You included some vocabulary words in the scene.	You included most vocabulary words in the scene.	You included all vocabulary words in the scene.
Vocabulary	You used no vocabulary words correctly.	You used few vocabulary words correctly.	You used some vocabulary words correctly.	You used most vocabulary words correctly.	You used all vocabulary words correctly.
Creativity	Your work does not show creativity or originality.	Your work shows little creativity or originality.	Your work is somewhat creative and original.	Your work is creative and original.	Your work is very creative and original.
Technology *(optional)*	You did not use technology or did not use it responsibly.	You may not have used technology or did not use it responsibly.	You attempted to use technology and used it responsibly.	You showed some ability to use technology responsibly and competently.	You used the technology responsibly and competently.

_____ /25

Teacher Comments: _____

_____

_____

_____

_____

_____

_____

_____

Science

The Water Cycle and Weather

Differentiation Strategy

 Menu of Options

Standards

- Students will understand that water exists in the air in different forms and changes from one form to another through various processes.

- TESOL: Students will use English to interact in the classroom.

Materials

- lesson resources (pages 96–99)

- art supplies

- books and websites on weather and the water cycle *(See page 167.)*

- video clip of weather interview *(optional)*

Procedures

❶ Display a colorful diagram of the water cycle. Discuss water's changes of state during the cycle. Explain evaporation, condensation, precipitation, and collection.

- *Evaporation* is the process by which water is changed from liquid to a gas or vapor.

- *Condensation* is the process by which water is changed from vapor to liquid.

- *Precipitation* is the discharge of water out of the atmosphere.

- *Collection* is the storage of water in oceans, lakes, snow, ice, and the atmosphere.

❷ Place students in four heterogeneous groups. Assign each group one of the steps of the water cycle. Have each group come up with a gesture to help everyone remember and understand its step of the water cycle. Have each group teach the whole class its gesture. Then, call out the steps as the whole class performs the corresponding gestures.

★ **English Language Support**—Interacting with vocabulary in this hands-on way will help English language learners recall key words. Posting the words with short, illustrated definitions will also help these students learn the lesson vocabulary.

❸ Have students think-pair-share answers to the following questions with partners seated nearby.

- *Does water ever become a solid during a weather event?*

- *What are some different types of storms and weather events, and what role does water play in each one?*

- *What extreme weather events have you experienced?*

❹ Have students choose partners for an interviewing activity. If possible, show students a video clip of a news reporter interviewing a subject about a weather event. Then, instruct partners to take turns interviewing each other about a weather event which they have experienced. If time allows, have volunteers conduct their interviews in front of the class.

The Water Cycle and Weather

5 Explain that people are often afraid of things that they do not understand. For some people, storms cause great anxiety. The next activity will allow students to learn more about a wide variety of weather events to better understand the science behind them. Explain to students that they will choose activities from *The Science of Storms Menu of Options* activity sheets (pages 96–97). Determine ahead of time how many points students need to complete from the menu, and set a due date for the projects. Have students use *The Science of Storms Project Planning Guide* activity sheet (page 98) while preparing to complete the activities.

6 If students finish early, they may complete the Anchor Activity.

Assessment

Use *The Science of Storms Rubric* (page 99) to assess students' work.

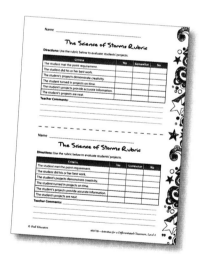

Anchor Activity

Have students research the linguistic origins of storm words, such as *tornado, hurricane, typhoon, monsoon, tsunami,* and *blizzard.*

Name _____

The Science of Storms Menu of Options

Directions: Choose projects from the list below. If you have a different project idea, you may propose it to your teacher. If accepted, it will be assigned a point value.

You must complete projects totaling _____ points.

Projects are due: _____

50-Point Projects
❏ **Snowflake Study:** Use books and websites to study snowflakes. Look for a connection between snowflakes and geometry. Create a presentation board that explains and gives examples of this math-science connection.
❏ **Meteorologist's Scrapbook:** Imagine you are a meteorologist who has experienced many major weather events. Make a scrapbook to share your experiences. Create two pages about each of the following types of storms: hurricanes, tornadoes, thunderstorms, and snowstorms. Include factual data, photos, and illustrations.
❏ **Interview a Storm Chaser:** Study the life of a real-life storm chaser. Then, pretend that you are a news reporter interviewing this person. Write your research in an interview format. Write questions and answer them as if the storm chaser were speaking about his or her life. Be sure to ask the subject about a time when he or she had a close call!

30-Point Projects
❏ **Build a Tornado Kit:** Find out what experts say should be included in a tornado kit. Ask an adult to help you gather the recommended items. Present the kit to the class. Be prepared to explain what each item is and its importance during or after a tornado.
❏ **Water-Cycle Traveler:** Imagine you are a tiny drop of water traveling through the water cycle. Write at least six journal entries about your exciting experiences. Include the following vocabulary words: *evaporation, condensation, precipitation,* and *collection.* Combine facts with creativity to write entries that are accurate and fun to read.
❏ **Hurricane Trading Cards:** Create a set of five historic hurricane trading cards. On one side of the card, write the name of a famous hurricane and its location. On the other side, list key facts about the storm, such as date, F-scale rating, damage caused, and wind speed.

 © *Shell Education*

The Science of Storms Menu of Options *(cont.)*

20-Point Projects
❑ **Storm Survey:** Conduct a storm survey. Ask at least 50 people which type of storm scares them most—tornado, hurricane, blizzard, tsunami, or thunderstorm. Take brief notes about the reason for each person's answer. Write a conclusion to explain the data.
❑ **Tornado Illustrations:** Research tornadoes and how they form. Use the information to illustrate the life of a typical tornado. Label each drawing with a description of what is happening.
❑ **Locate Tornado Alley:** Where is Tornado Alley? Research this storm-chasing hot spot. Then, design a map that shows its location. Include at least six other facts about or points of interest in Tornado Alley on the map.

10-Point Projects
❑ **Lightning Poster:** What is lightning? Answer this question with facts from books and websites. Make a poster to show what you learned. The design of your poster should catch people's attention. The facts should teach them something interesting.
❑ **Storm Art:** Use any medium (paint, clay, recycled objects) to create a piece of art that conveys your feelings about storms.
❑ **Hurricanes vs. Tornadoes:** Make a T-chart comparing hurricanes and tornadoes. Include at least six facts about each type of storm.

Student-Proposed Projects
❑ _____   _____   _____   _____   ❑ _____   _____   _____   _____

Name _____

The Science of Storms
Project Planning Guide

Directions: Complete the chart below to help plan your projects.

You must complete projects totaling _____ points.

Projects are due: _____

Project Name	Points	Resources Needed
Total Points:		

Name _____

The Science of Storms Rubric

Directions: Use the rubric below to evaluate students' projects.

Criteria	Yes	Somewhat	No
The student met the point requirement.			
The student did his or her best work.			
The student's projects demonstrate creativity.			
The student turned in projects on time.			
The student's projects provide accurate information.			
The student's projects are neat.			

Teacher Comments: _____

_____

_____

_____

– –

Name _____

The Science of Storms Rubric

Directions: Use the rubric below to evaluate students' projects.

Criteria	Yes	Somewhat	No
The student met the point requirement.			
The student did his or her best work.			
The student's projects demonstrate creativity.			
The student turned in projects on time.			
The student's projects provide accurate information.			
The student's projects are neat.			

Teacher Comments: _____

_____

_____

_____

The Moon

Differentiation Strategy

 Choices Board

Standards

- Students will know that Earth is one of several planets that orbit the sun and that the moon orbits Earth.
- TESOL: Students will use English to obtain, process, construct, and provide subject matter information in spoken and written form.

Materials

- lesson resources (pages 102–105)
- chart paper and markers
- video clip or photos of the moon
- sticky notes
- books and websites about the moon and solar system *(See page 167.)*
- audio recorder
- art supplies

Procedures

Preparation Note: Make a large *KWL* chart. Display the chart in the classroom where students can reach it.

❶ Begin the lesson by showing students a short video clip or photos of the moon. Ask students to think about what they already know about the moon. Distribute several sticky notes to each student. Have students write down things that they know, or think that they know, about the moon. Invite them to post the sticky notes in the *K* column (what students *know*) of the *KWL* chart.

❷ Ask students to use the sticky notes to write down things they want to know about the moon. Invite them to post these in the *W* column (what students *want* to know) of the *KWL* chart.

❸ Explain to students that the *L* column (what students *learned*) will remain empty for now. As students learn new information about the moon, they will write it on sticky notes to post in the *L* column.

❹ Read the posted sticky notes aloud. Do not evaluate students' ideas at this point; simply share the information with a focus on generating interest and engaging background knowledge.

❺ Explain to students that they will have a chance to answer some of their questions about the moon. Assign students a shape based on their readiness levels.

❻ Distribute *The Mysterious Moon Choices Board* activity sheet (page 102) to students. Tell students that they will complete two activities that match the shape you assign to them. Another option is to distribute *The Mysterious Moon Choices Cards* (pages 103–105) to students based on readiness levels. This will allow them to see activities at their levels only. These activities will involve independent research. (This could also be used as a week-long homework project.) Note that one card encourages students to propose their own research question.

★ **English Language Support**—Meet with your English language learners and read the choices aloud to them. Have students make audio recordings of their work, or meet with them to help them put their ideas into writing.

The Moon

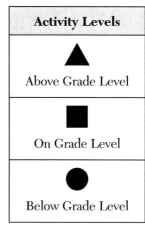

7 As students research, remind them to add sticky notes to the *L* column of the *KWL* chart to share and reinforce their learning.

8 When the students complete their activities, review the *K* column of the chart to confirm students' knowledge and the *W* column to be sure all questions were answered.

9 If students finish early, they may complete the Anchor Activity.

Assessment

Have students complete an exit slip by responding to this question in writing: *What are three things you learned about the moon during this lesson?* Evaluate students' responses to determine whether or not the lesson objective was met

Activity Levels
▲
Above Grade Level
■
On Grade Level
●
Below Grade Level

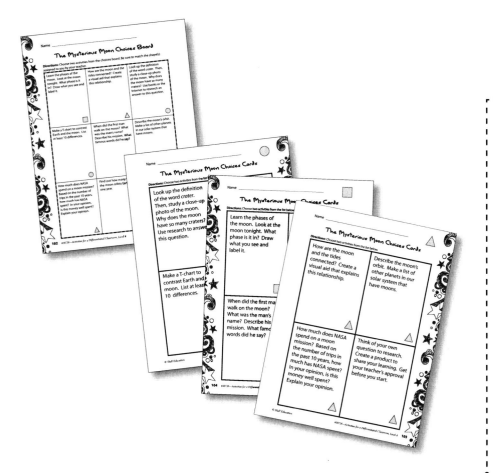

Anchor Activity

Have students research legends and folktales about the moon. Ask them to compare and contrast two or more stories. Have students think about why the stories were told and what they say about people's feelings about the moon.

Name _____

The Mysterious Moon Choices Board

Directions: Choose two activities from the choices board. Be sure to match the shape(s) assigned to you by your teacher.

Learn the phases of the moon. Look at the moon tonight. In what phase is it? Draw what you see and label it. ▫	How are the moon and the tides connected? Create a visual aid that explains this relationship. △	Look up the definition of the word *crater*. Then, study a close-up photo of the moon. Why does the moon have so many craters? Use books or the Internet to research an answer to this question. ○
Make a T-chart to contrast Earth and the moon. List at least 10 differences. ○	When did the first man walk on the moon? What was the man's name? Describe his mission. What famous words did he say? ▫	Describe the moon's orbit. Make a list of other planets in our solar system that have moons. △
How much does NASA spend on a moon mission? Based on the number of trips in the past 10 years, how much has NASA spent? In your opinion, is this money well spent? Explain your opinion. △	Find out how many times the moon orbits Earth in one year. ○	How many miles is the moon from Earth? How long does the trip take? Compare this to other trips on Earth. For example, find out how long it would take you to travel from New York City, USA, to Paris, France. Create a visual aid to show your findings. ▫

Name _____

The Mysterious Moon Choices Cards

Directions: Choose two activities from the list below.

How are the moon and the tides connected? Create a visual aid that explains this relationship.	Describe the moon's orbit. Make a list of other planets in our solar system that have moons.
How much does NASA spend on a moon mission? Based on the number of trips in the past 10 years, how much has NASA spent? In your opinion, is this money well spent? Explain your opinion.	Think of your own question to research. Create a product to share your learning. Get your teacher's approval before you start.

Name _____

The Mysterious Moon Choices Cards

Directions: Choose two activities from the list below.

Learn the phases of the moon. Look at the moon tonight. In what phase is it? Draw what you see and label it.	How many miles is the moon from Earth? How long does the trip take? Compare this to other trips on Earth. For example, find out how long it would take you to travel from New York City, USA, to Paris, France. Create a visual aid to show your findings.
When did the first man walk on the moon? What was the man's name? Describe his mission. What famous words did he say?	Think of your own question to research. Create a product to share your learning. Get your teacher's approval before you start.

Name _____

The Mysterious Moon Choices Cards

Directions: Choose two activities from the list below.

Look up the definition of the word *crater*. Then, study a close-up photo of the moon. Why does the moon have so many craters? Use research to answer this question.	Find out how many times the moon orbits Earth in one year.
Make a T-chart to contrast Earth and the moon. List at least 10 differences.	Think of your own question to research. Create a product to share your learning. Get your teacher's approval before you start.

States of Matter

Differentiation Strategy

 Tiered Assignments

Standards

- Students will understand that matter has different states and that each state has distinct physical properties; some common materials such as water can be changed from one state to another by heating or cooling.

- TESOL: Students will use English to obtain, process, construct, and provide subject matter information in spoken and written form.

Materials

- lesson resources (pages 108–111)

- audio recorder *(optional)*

Procedures

1 Have students each make a three-column chart on a sheet of paper. Label the columns *solids*, *liquids*, and *gases*. To see what students already know about the states of matter, send them on a scavenger hunt for examples to record in each column.

2 After the scavenger hunt, allow students to share their examples. This will show you what they know about the states of matter. Ask students to check their lists against the definitions you are about to give to them, and edit their lists accordingly.

3 Display and discuss the definitions of the three states of matter. Explain the properties of matter in each state.

- *Solids* have stable, definite shapes and definite volumes. Their molecules are packed tightly together. Solids can only change shape by force, such as being broken or cut.

- *Liquids* do not have a definite shape. Their shapes are determined by their containers. Their molecules are not as tightly packed as the molecules of a solid. They are pourable.

- *Gases* have no definite shape or volume but fill whatever container they occupy. Their molecules are loosely structured and can move freely.

4 Have students act out each state of matter. As solids, students should stand close together with shoulders nearly touching. Ask students to try to fit through the classroom door in this formation. It is impossible without breaking the structure. As liquids, students should stand close together without touching. They can fit through the classroom door by rearranging their formation. As gases, students should stand in a loose grouping. They can fit through the classroom door without any problem. They have room to move freely. Have them come back inside the classroom and spread out to fill the room, just as a gas would fill a container.

5 Assign students a shape based on their readiness levels.

States of Matter

6 Distribute the *What's the Matter?* activity sheets (pages 108–110) to students based on their readiness levels. Provide time for them to complete the activities independently.

★ **English Language Support**—This activity requires a significant amount of reading. Place English language learners in the circle group. Read the passage aloud to the students in this group who need the additional support (or make an audio recording of the passage for them to listen to). Guide students as they answer the questions collaboratively. Model how to scan the passage for answers to the questions.

Activity Levels
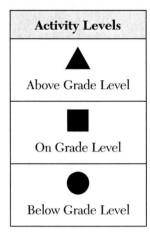
Above Grade Level
■
On Grade Level
●
Below Grade Level

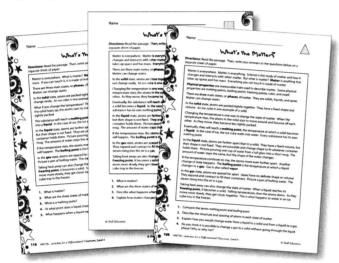

7 As an extension, divide the class into heterogeneous groups to continue exploring states of matter. Distribute the *Changing States of Matter Extension* activity sheet (page 111). Read the directions aloud to the class and have students complete the activities in their new groups.

8 If students finish early, they may complete the Anchor Activity.

Assessment

Assess students' understanding of states of matter by evaluating their answers at the bottom of their activity sheets. Plan reteaching lessons for small groups, as necessary.

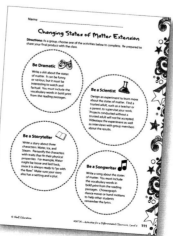

Anchor Activity

Have students find out the name and properties of the fourth state of matter *(plasma)*. Have them make a short presentation on it for the class.

Name _____

What's the Matter?

Directions: Read the passage. Then, write your answers to the questions below on a separate sheet of paper.

Matter is everywhere. Matter is everything. Science is the study of matter and how it changes and interacts with other matter. But what is matter? **Matter** is anything that takes up space and has mass. Everything you can touch is made of matter.

Physical properties are measurable traits used to describe matter. Some physical properties are melting points, boiling points, freezing points, color, and smell.

There are three main states, or **phases**, of matter. They are solids, liquids, and gases. Matter can change states.

In the **solid** state, atoms are packed tightly together. They have a fixed shape and volume. An ice cube is one example of a solid.

Changing the temperature is one way to change the state of matter. When the temperature rises, the atoms in the solid start to move around and bounce off each other. As they move, they become less tightly packed.

Eventually, they will reach a **melting point**, the temperature at which a solid becomes a **liquid**. In the case of ice, the ice cube melts into water. Every substance has its own melting point.

In the **liquid** state, atoms are farther apart than in a solid. They have a fixed volume, but their shape is not fixed. They are pourable and change shape to fit whatever container holds them. Picture pouring one cup of water from a tall glass into a short mug. The amount of water stays the same, but the shape of the water changes.

If the temperature continues to rise, the atoms move even farther apart. Another change of state happens. The **boiling point** is the temperature at which a liquid changes to a **gas**. Gas is also called **vapor**.

In the **gas** state, atoms are spaced far apart. Gases have no definite shape or volume. They expand and contract to fill their containers. Picture a pan of boiling water. The steam rising into the air is a gas.

Taking heat away can also change the state of matter. When a liquid reaches its **freezing point**, it becomes a solid. Falling temperatures slow the atoms down. As they move more slowly, they get closer together. This is what happens to water in an ice cube tray in the freezer.

1. Compare the terms *melting point* and *boiling point*.

2. Describe the structure and spacing of atoms in each state of matter.

3. Explain how you would change water from a liquid to a solid and from a liquid to a gas.

4. Do you think it is possible to change a gas to a solid without going through the liquid phase? Why or why not?

© *Shell Education*

Name _____

What's the Matter?

Directions: Read the passage. Then, write your answers to the questions below on a separate sheet of paper.

Matter is everywhere. Matter is everything. Science is the study of matter and how it changes and interacts with other matter. But what is matter? **Matter** is anything that takes up space and has mass. Everything you can touch is made of matter.

There are three main states, or **phases**, of matter. They are solids, liquids, and gases. Matter can change states.

In the **solid** state, atoms are close together. They have a shape and volume that does not change easily. An ice cube is one example of a solid.

Changing the temperature is one way to change the state of matter. When the temperature rises, the atoms in the solid start to move around and bounce off each other. As they move, they become less tightly packed.

Eventually, the substance will reach a **melting point**. This is the temperature at which a solid becomes a **liquid**. In the case of ice, the ice cube melts into water. Every substance has its own melting point.

In the **liquid** state, atoms are farther apart than in a solid. They have a fixed volume, but their shape is not fixed. They are pourable. They change shape to fit whatever container holds them. Picture pouring one cup of water from a tall glass into a short mug. The amount of water stays the same, but the shape of the water changes.

If the temperature rises, the atoms move even farther apart. Another change of state will happen. The **boiling point** is the temperature at which a liquid changes to a **gas**.

In the **gas** state, atoms are spaced far apart. Gases have no definite shape or volume. They expand and contract to fill their containers. Picture a pan of boiling water. The steam rising into the air is a gas.

Taking heat away can also change the state of matter. When a liquid reaches its **freezing point**, it becomes a solid. Falling temperatures slow the atoms down. As they move more slowly, they get closer together. This is what happens to water in an ice cube tray in the freezer.

1. What is matter?

2. What are the three states of matter?

3. Describe what happens when the temperature of a solid is increased.

4. Explain how matter changes from a liquid to a solid.

Name _____

What's the Matter?

Directions: Read the passage. Then, write your answers to the questions below on a separate sheet of paper.

Matter is everywhere. What is matter? **Matter** is anything that takes up space and has mass. If you can touch it, it is made of matter

There are three main states, or **phases**, of matter. They are solids, liquids, and gases. Matter can change states.

In the **solid** state, atoms are packed tight. They have a shape and volume that does not change easily. An ice cube is one example of a solid.

What if you change the temperature? That is one way to change the state of matter. As the solid heats up, the atoms start to move around. As they move, they become less tightly packed.

The substance will reach a **melting point**. This is the temperature at which a solid turns into a **liquid**. In the case of ice, the ice cube melts into water.

In the **liquid** state, atoms are farther apart than in a solid. They have a fixed volume. But their shape is not fixed. They are pourable. They change shape to fit whatever container holds them. Picture pouring one cup of water from a tall glass into a short mug. The amount of water stays the same, but the shape of the water changes.

If the temperature rises, the atoms move even farther apart. Another change of state will happen. The **boiling point** is the temperature at which a liquid changes to a **gas**.

In the **gas** state, atoms are spaced far apart. Gases have no definite shape or volume. Picture a pan of boiling water. The steam rising into the air is a gas.

Taking heat away can also change the state of matter. When a liquid reaches its **freezing point**, it becomes a solid. Falling temperatures slow the atoms down. As they move more slowly, they get closer together. This is what happens to water in an ice cube tray in the freezer.

1. What is matter?

2. What are the three states of matter?

3. What is a melting point?

4. At what point does a liquid change to a gas?

5. What happens when a liquid reaches its freezing point?

© *Shell Education*

Name _____

Changing States of Matter Extension

Directions: As a group, choose one of the activities below to complete. Be prepared to share your final product with the class.

Be Dramatic

Write a skit about the states of matter. It can be funny or serious, but it must be interesting to watch and factual. You must include the vocabulary words in bold print from the reading passages.

Be a Scientist

Design an experiment to learn more about the states of matter. Find a trusted adult, such as a teacher or a parent, to supervise your work. Projects conducted without a trusted adult will not be accepted. Videotape the experiment as well as interviews with group members about the results.

Be a Storyteller

Write a story about three characters: Water, Ice, and Steam. Personify the characters with traits that fit their physical properties. For example, Water might be loose and laid back, since it is always ready to "go with the flow." Make sure your story also has a setting and a plot.

Be a Songwriter

Write a song about the states of matter. You must include the vocabulary words in bold print from the reading passages. Choreograph dance moves or hand motions to help other students remember the lyrics.

Science

Life Cycles

Differentiation Strategy

 Tiered Graphic Organizers

Standards

- Students will understand that animals progress through life cycles of birth, growth and development, reproduction, and death; the details of these life cycles are different for different organisms.
- TESOL: Students will use English to obtain, process, construct, and provide subject matter information in spoken and written form.

Materials

- lesson resources (pages 114–117)
- books and websites with information about frog, salmon, and grasshopper life cycles *(See page 167.)*
- books and websites about animals *(See page 167.)*

Procedures

1 Ask students to share what they know about life cycles. Explain that this means how animals are born and how they grow. Invite volunteers to share ideas about life cycles in general.

2 Divide the class into five heterogeneous groups. Explain that each group will prepare a short skit that acts out the life cycle of a butterfly. Give students time to prepare a simple skit. Students should base their skits on background knowledge alone; research is not necessary at this point. If building background knowledge on the life cycle of a butterfly is necessary for students, you may distribute the butterfly life cycle reference card (page 117).

3 Have each group perform its skit. Compliment each group's thinking and resist the urge to correct misconceptions at this point.

4 After all groups have performed, lead a discussion about the similarities and differences among animal life cycles. Correct any misconceptions at this time.

5 Explain that students will complete a graphic organizer that shows the life cycle of either a frog, a grasshopper, or a salmon.

6 Distribute the *Life Cycle Comparisons* activity sheets (pages 114–116) to students based on their readiness levels. Allow students to choose partners with the same activity sheet. These pairs should use various resources to find out about the life cycles of their animals and then record them on their graphic organizers. Have the students wait to complete the written response at the bottom of their activity sheets.

★ **English Language Support**—Place English language learners with partners based on their science abilities. The diagrams on the activity sheets should provide some language support. If necessary, review with the partners of these students how to effectively work with English language learners. Remind them that despite a language barrier, these students have ideas to contribute. Suggest that they allow extra time for their partners to explain ideas and help them pronounce new words, if necessary.

 © *Shell Education*

Life Cycles

7 Once students finish their graphic organizers, divide the class into small heterogeneous groups and let students share their graphic organizers with their groups. Be sure your below-grade-level students have homogeneous partners so they can support each other as they share their work. While in these heterogeneous groups, students should complete the written response at the bottom of their graphic organizers.

8 As an extension, have students research the life cycles of two additional animals of their choice. Provide books and websites for students to use independently. Have students create a graphic organizer to compare and contrast the life cycles of two or more animals.

9 If students finish early, they may complete the Anchor Activity.

Assessment

Evaluate students' graphic organizers and written responses to see if they have learned the concepts taught in this lesson. Use the *Life Cycle Reference Cards* (page 117) to check students' work. You may also distribute these cards to students so that they can check their own work.

Activity Levels
▲
Above Grade Level
■
On Grade Level
●
Below Grade Level

Anchor Activity

Have students compile a fact file about the life cycles of different classes of animals. Students should study the life cycles of amphibians, birds, fish, insects, mammals, and reptiles, and use research and creativity to produce a fact file of information that other students will want to read.

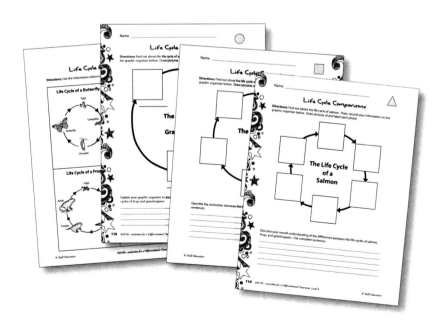

Name _____

Life Cycle Comparisons

Directions: Find out about the life cycle of salmon. Then, record your information on the graphic organizer below. Draw pictures of and label each phase.

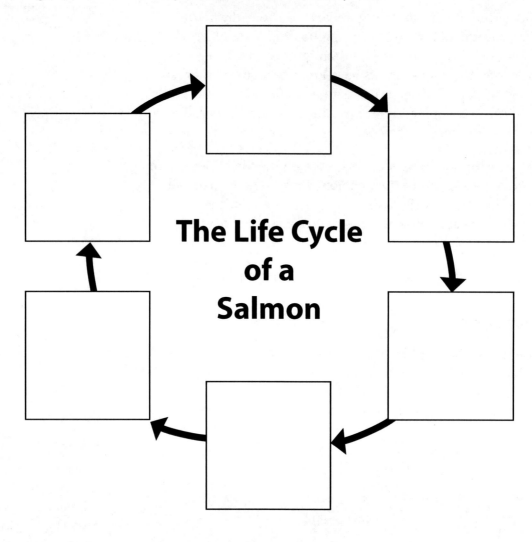

The Life Cycle of a Salmon

Describe your overall understanding of the differences between the life cycles of salmon, frogs, and grasshoppers. Use complete sentences.

_____

_____

_____

_____

_____

    © *Shell Education*

Name _____

Life Cycle Comparisons

Directions: Find out about the life cycle of a frog. Then, record your information on the graphic organizer below. Draw pictures of and label each phase.

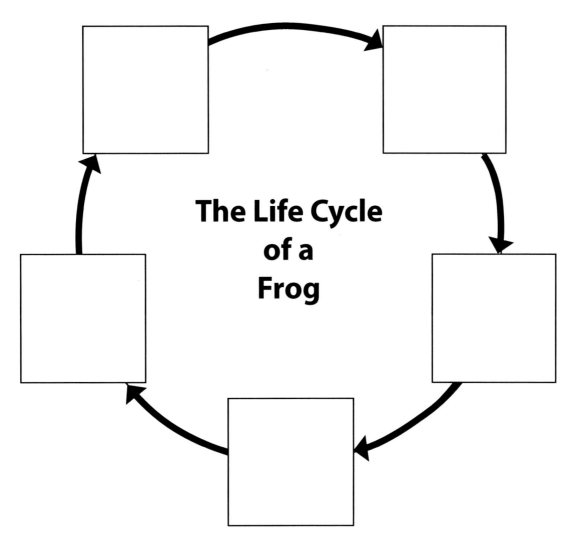

The Life Cycle of a Frog

Describe the similarities between the life cycles of frogs and grasshoppers. Use complete sentences.

_____

_____

_____

_____

_____

Name _____

Life Cycle Comparisons

Directions: Find out about the life cycle of a grasshopper. Then, record your information on the graphic organizer below. Draw pictures and label each phase.

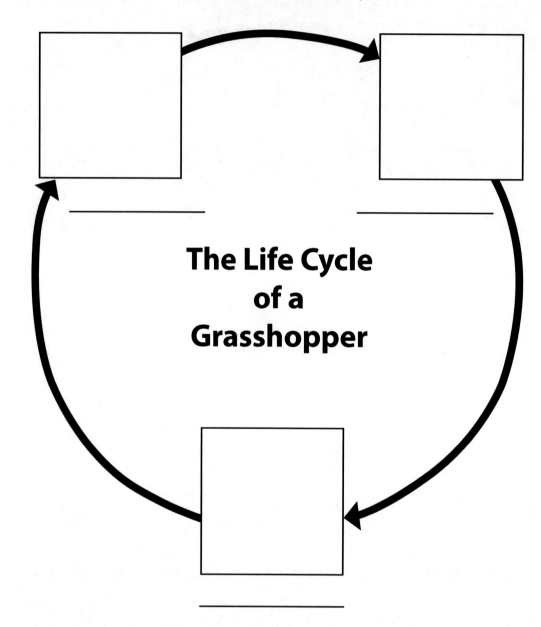

The Life Cycle of a Grasshopper

Explain your graphic organizer to your teacher. Also, explain the similarities between the life cycles of frogs and grasshoppers.

_____

_____

_____

_____

© *Shell Education*

Life Cycle Reference Cards

Directions: Use the information below to check students' graphic organizers.

Life Cycle of a Butterfly

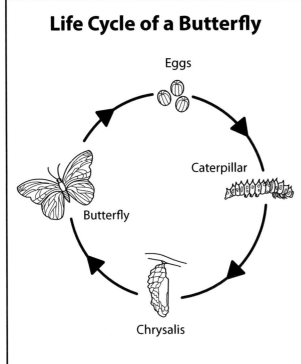

Life Cycle of a Salmon

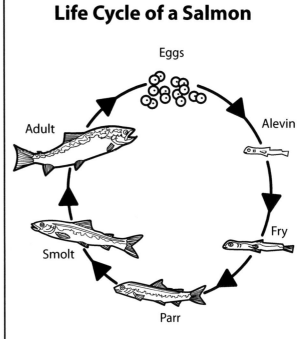

Life Cycle of a Frog

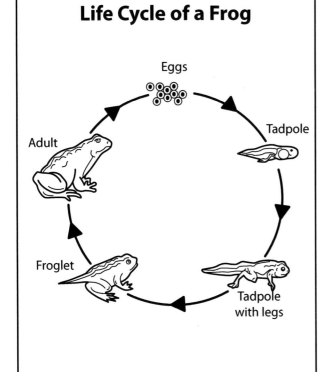

Life Cycle of a Grasshopper

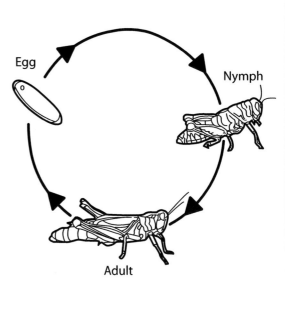

© Shell Education

How Animals Adapt

Differentiation Strategy

 Multiple Intelligences

Standards

• Students will understand that an organism's patterns of behavior are related to the nature of that organism's environment.

• TESOL: Students will use appropriate learning strategies to construct and apply academic knowledge.

Materials

• *lesson resources (pages 120–123)*

• 3 bowls

• grapes

• uncooked rice

• water

• tongs

• tweezers

• toothpicks

• coffee stirrers

• video clips or photos of birds feeding *(See page 167.)*

• Internet

• audio recorder

Procedures

Preparation Note: Place the grapes in one bowl, uncooked rice in another, and water in a third bowl. Display the three bowls where all students can see them and reach them. Set out tongs, tweezers, toothpicks, and coffee stirrers near the bowls.

1 Begin the lesson by asking student volunteers to help you. Hand one student the tongs and ask him or her (with a serious face) to use the tongs to get you some water. Look puzzled when the student does not succeed. Hand another student a coffee stirrer and ask him or her to get you some rice. Again, look confused when this fails. Finally, hand a third student a pair of tweezers and ask him or her to pick up some grapes (no stabbing allowed). Again, look puzzled when this does not work.

2 Look at the class and ask dramatically how you will ever be able to get what you need with these tools. Explain that you can only use each tool for one of the items to avoid contamination. Ask for help figuring out which tool works best with which item. Allow volunteers to come up and show the class how to use tongs to pick up grapes, a stirrer to suck up water, and tweezers to pick up grains of rice.

3 Explain to students that these specialized tools are similar to the beaks of some birds. These birds have beaks that are specially suited for the type of food that they eat. Explain to students how hummingbirds, warblers, and pelicans use their beaks for survival.

• Hummingbirds use their long, narrow beaks to reach deep inside flowers to drink the nectar. This is similar to the coffee stirrers and the water.

• Warblers use their short, narrow beaks to reach into tight places, such as between the bark of tree trunks to eat tiny insects. This is similar to the tweezers and the rice.

• Pelicans have some of the longest beaks in the bird world. They use their long beaks to scoop up fish underwater. A pouch at the bottom of the beak expands to help the pelican swallow large fish. This is similar to the tongs and the grapes.

How Animals Adapt

★ **English Language Support**—Display photos or show video clips of hummingbirds, warblers, and pelicans feeding. This will help the English language learners better understand the lesson and learn the new vocabulary.

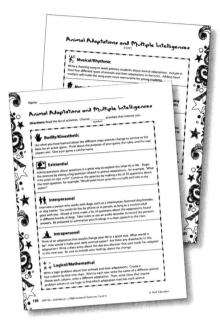

4 Explain that the beaks of these birds are examples of animal adaptations. An *adaptation* is a change to an animal or plant that makes it easier for it to exist in its environment. Ask students to brainstorm other examples of animal adaptations. List these on the board.

5 Tell students that they will now learn more about animal adaptations by choosing projects that fit their interests. Distribute the *Animal Adaptations and Multiple Intelligences* activity sheets (pages 120–121) to students. Review the activity options with the class and assign students a specific number of activities to complete, independently or with partners who share the same interests. Determine a due date for the projects.

6 Distribute the *Brainstorming Idea Catcher* activity sheet (page 122) to help students get started on their projects. Provide students with one sheet for each project that they will complete. Remind students that in brainstorming, they should put down any ideas that come to mind without judging them. Tell students that great ideas come from unexpected sources, including thoughts that may at first seem silly or impossible.

Anchor Activity

Have students research human adaptations. Then, have them imagine human adaptations that might occur in the future. Ask students to draw and label a picture of a "human of the future" and his or her adaptations.

7 If students finish early, they may complete the Anchor Activity.

Assessment

Use the *Animal Adaptations Activities Rubric* (page 123) to assess students' work. Use one rubric for each student project.

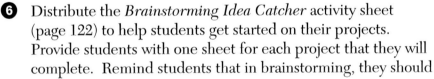

Name _____

Animal Adaptations and Multiple Intelligences

Directions: Read the list of activities. Choose _____ activities that interest you.

(number)

 Bodily/Kinesthetic

Use what you have learned about the different ways animals change to survive as the basis for an active game. Think about the purpose of your game, the rules, and the way players win. Give your game a catchy name.

 Existential

Asking questions about questions is a great way to explore the what-ifs in life. Begin this exercise by asking a big question related to animal adaptations, for example, *"What if the polar ice caps melt?"* Continue the exercise by making a list of 20 questions about the main question, for example, *"Would polar bears grow fins and gills and take to the water?"*

 Interpersonal

Interview a person who works with dogs, such as a veterinarian, licensed dog breeder, or dog trainer. You could do this by phone or in person, as long as a trusted adult goes with you. Ahead of time, make a list of questions about the adaptations found in different breeds of dogs. Take notes or use an audio recorder to record the person's answers. Be prepared to summarize your findings in a short speech to the class.

 Intrapersonal

Think of an adaptation that would change your life in a good way. What would it be? How would it make your daily survival easier? Are there any drawbacks to this adaptation? Write a diary entry about the day you discover that your body has adapted in this new way. Be sure to include your feelings about the change.

+ −
× ÷ **Logical/Mathematical**

Write a logic problem about four animals and their adaptations. Create a four-column by four-row chart. Next to each row, write the name of a different animal. Above each column, write a different adaptation. Then, write clues that require problem solvers to use logic to find which adaptation matches each animal.

Animal Adaptations and Multiple Intelligences
(cont.)

 Musical/Rhythmic

Write a rhyming song to teach primary students about animal adaptations. Include in the lyrics at least four different types of animals and their adaptations. Adding hand motions will make the song even more memorable for young students.

 Naturalist

Research the special adaptations of two endangered animals. Find out what is being done to save these species from extinction. Make a colorful poster that will educate others about these special animals.

 Verbal/Linguistic

Write a speech to give to the class about the adaptations of two animals. Explain how these adaptations help the animals survive in their specific habitats. Include photos or illustrations of the animals to use as visual aids.

 Visual/Spatial

Choose an animal that interests you. Imagine how it would have to adapt to survive in a completely different habitat. For example, a polar bear could use stripes to hide in the jungle and an alligator would need a coat of heavy fur to survive in the arctic. Draw a colorful illustration of the animal in its new environment. Your picture should clearly show the animal's adaptations.

My Action Plan

I plan to complete the following project or projects:

_____

_____

I will need to take these steps to complete my work:

_____

_____

_____

Projects are due: _____

Name _____

Brainstorming Idea Catcher

Directions: The best way to begin any project is with a great idea! Start this project by spending some time brainstorming about your topic and project ideas. In the box below, make a web or a list to brainstorm topic ideas.

Directions: Choose a topic from the web above. In the box below, make a web or a list of ideas for your project. For example, if you plan to invent a game, start listing games you love to play. If you want to conduct an interview, list people and places you might want to call.

Name _____

Animal Adaptations Activities Rubric

Reading the Rubric: Your project has been graded on five criteria. You earned a score from 1 to 5 for each item. Your project is worth a total of 25 points.

Criteria	Poor	Needs Work	Fair	Strong	Excellent
You followed project guidelines.	1	2	3	4	5
You demonstrated knowledge of adaptations.	1	2	3	4	5
Your facts are accurate.	1	2	3	4	5
Your ideas are original and creative.	1	2	3	4	5
Your work is neat and careful.	1	2	3	4	5
				Score	____ /25

Teacher Comments: _____

_____

— —

Name _____

Animal Adaptations Activities Rubric

Reading the Rubric: Your project has been graded on five criteria. You earned a score from 1 to 5 for each item. Your project is worth a total of 25 points.

Criteria	Poor	Needs Work	Fair	Strong	Excellent
You followed project guidelines.	1	2	3	4	5
You demonstrated knowledge of adaptations.	1	2	3	4	5
Your facts are accurate.	1	2	3	4	5
Your ideas are original and creative.	1	2	3	4	5
Your work is neat and careful.	1	2	3	4	5
				Score	____ /25

Teacher Comments: _____

_____

Erosion

Differentiation Strategy

Leveled Questions

Standards

- Students will understand how features on Earth's surface are constantly changed by a combination of slow and rapid processes.
- TESOL: Students will use appropriate learning strategies to extend their sociolinguistic and sociocultural competence.

Materials

- lesson resources (pages 126–129)
- index cards
- books and websites about erosion *(See page 167.)*

Procedures

Preparation Note: Write the following types of erosion and weathering on index cards: *water erosion, wind erosion, glacial erosion, coastal erosion, weathering,* and *mass wasting* . If you plan to divide the class into six groups, make two sets of cards. If you would rather have 12 smaller groups, make four sets of cards.

1 Display the dramatic photos of weathering and erosion on *Examples of Erosion* (pages 126–127.) These images are also available on the Teacher Resource CD in color. Ask students to study the landforms in the photos and imagine how they were created. Have students think-pair-share their ideas with classmates seated nearby.

2 Explain to students that *erosion* is the term used to describe the processes that break down rocks and carry away the broken pieces. There are several types of erosion. Explain that the photos show the effects of erosion on the earth.

3 Divide the class into heterogeneous groups. Distribute one index card labeled with an erosion term (see Preparation Note) to each group. Explain that each group is responsible for teaching the rest of the class about its topic. Distribute the *Erosion Guide* activity sheet (page 128) to students. Read the directions aloud to the whole class. Show students the resources available for research. Allow time for them to gather the necessary facts.

❹ Provide necessary support as groups find and prepare photos for use as visual aids.

★ **English Language Support**—Assign English language learners the task of collecting photos in their groups. Serving in this important role is a way for these students to contribute in a significant way and to build confidence.

❺ After students complete their research, have each group present to the class. Ask the class to listen carefully to each presentation for facts to record on their *Erosion Guide* activity sheet (page 128). Provide support during the presentations to make sure that the presenters include essential information. Fill in any gaps and correct misconceptions so that students record information correctly on their activity sheets.

❻ Distribute the *Erosion Essential Questions* activity sheet (page 129) to students based on their readiness levels. Have students work with partners who have the same shape.

❼ If students finish early, they may complete the Anchor Activity.

Assessment

Use the students' responses to the *Erosion Essential Questions* to assess what students have learned about erosion.

Activity Levels
▲
Above Grade Level
■
On Grade Level
●
Below Grade Level

Anchor Activity

Have students design erosion experiments. Instruct them to begin by asking a specific question about erosion and answering the question with a hypothesis. They should proceed by following the steps of the Scientific Process to carry out their experiments.

Examples of Erosion

Antelope Canyon
Arizona, U.S.A.
Wind and Water Erosion

Arbol de Piedra (Stone Tree)
Altiplano, Bolivia
Wind Erosion

 © *Shell Education*

Examples of Erosion *(cont.)*

**Half Dome
Yosemite, California, U.S.A.
Glacial Erosion**

**Hidden Lake
Glacier National Park, Montana, U.S.A.
Glacial Erosion**

**Beach Road, Happisburgh
Norfolk, England
Coastal Erosion**

**Cathedral Cove Beach
Coromandel, North Island, New Zealand
Water Erosion**

Name _____

Erosion Guide

Part 1

Directions: Work with your group to research your erosion vocabulary term. Complete the top section of this activity sheet together.

Vocabulary term: _____

Definition: _____

_____

Description: _____

_____

_____

Examples: _____

_____

_____

List the book titles and page numbers or Web pages where you found photos that clearly illustrate your vocabulary term:

_____

_____

Part 2

Directions: Listen carefully as your classmates explain the meanings of their vocabulary terms. Record the key facts below.

1. Vocabulary term: _____

Description: _____

_____

2. Vocabulary term: _____

Description: _____

_____

3. Vocabulary term: _____

Description: _____

_____

4. Vocabulary term: _____

Description: _____

_____

5. Vocabulary term: _____

Description: _____

_____

Name _____

Erosion Essential Questions

Directions: Discuss the questions with your partner. Then, answer the questions on your own on a separate sheet of paper. Make sure to write your answers in complete sentences.

1. Explain the connection between weathering and erosion.

2. Describe the four main types of erosion.

3. Which type of erosion is responsible for most of Earth's reshaping? Explain the reason for this.

— —

Name _____

Erosion Essential Questions

Directions: Discuss the questions with your partner. Then, answer the questions on your own on a separate sheet of paper. Make sure to write your answers in complete sentences.

1. Describe how weathering and erosion work together.

2. List and define the four main types of erosion.

3. Which type of erosion has the greatest effect on the earth? Explain why.

— —

Name _____

Erosion Essential Questions

Directions: Work with your partner to answer the questions below.

1. What is weathering? _____
   _____

2. What is erosion? _____
   _____

3. What are four types of erosion? _____
   _____
   _____

4. What do you know about water erosion? Write what you know in the space below.
   _____
   _____

Map Skills

Differentiation Strategy

 Tiered Assignments

Standards

• Students will understand the basic elements of maps and globes.

• TESOL: Students will use appropriate learning strategies to construct and apply academic knowledge.

Materials

• lesson resources (pages 132–135)

• maps of different styles

• clipboards, one for every two students

• scissors

• index cards

• glue sticks

• Internet

• art supplies

Procedures

Preparation Note: Post a wide variety of maps around the classroom at student eye level. Include maps of shopping malls, amusement parks, hotels, and other attractions in addition to the typical world, country, state, and city maps.

1 Allow students to choose partners for a map exploration. Instruct students to walk around the classroom and study the maps. Encourage them to appreciate each map's unique qualities and artistry. Ask students to each choose a favorite map and explain their choices to their partners.

2 Distribute a clipboard and lined paper to each pair of students. Ask them to examine all of the maps in the classroom a second time. This time, they should pay special attention to the features that the maps have in common. On the lined paper, they should list the common features.

3 Bring students back together for a whole-class discussion. As students report their findings, add the features to a class list on the board. This list should include some mention of the following (even though students might not know the correct terms yet)—*title, compass rose, map legend, scale, grid,* and *latitude* and *longitude lines.*

4 Distribute the *Map Skills Vocabulary Matchup* activity sheet (page 132) to each student. Explain that the words and definitions need to be matched up correctly. Ask students to cut apart the words and definitions. Then, have them use background knowledge and educated guesses to match words with definitions.

★ **English Language Support**—Point out the features on a map as you pronounce each word several times. Invite students to practice saying the words. Then, read each definition aloud slowly and clearly. Encourage students to make educated guesses as they try to match the words and definitions.

5 Give each student eight index cards. On the board or projector, show students the correct vocabulary matchups. Discuss each term and point out examples on the maps.

Map Skills

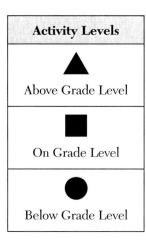

6 Model for students how to glue the word to one side of an index card and the definition on the other side. This will make vocabulary flash cards that students can use to review word meanings.

7 Play a simple map game with the whole class. Call two students to the front of the room. Challenge them to find a specific location on one of the maps. Ask questions that require students to use the grid system, map directions, map legends, and other vocabulary terms. The student who finds the location first wins the round. The loser must return to his or her seat while the winner plays against another student. The game continues until every student has had a turn.

8 Explain to students that they will now make maps. Distribute the *Make a Map* activity sheets (pages 133–135) to students based on their readiness levels. Give English language learners the sheets that best match their individual readiness. Read the directions aloud to each group of students. For added support, partner students within the readiness groups.

9 Begin the project by taking each group on a walk around the area that it will map. The above-grade-level students will map the neighborhood where the school is located. They might benefit from using Google™ Earth. The on-grade-level students will map the school. Your below-grade-level students will map the classroom. Allow students time to complete their maps. Then, display them in the classroom when they are completed.

10 If students finish early, they may complete the Anchor Activity.

Assessment

Evaluate the maps that students create to assess their understanding of the concepts taught.

Activity Levels
▲
Above Grade Level
■
On Grade Level
●
Below Grade Level

Anchor Activity

Have students research historically significant maps. Suggest that they look up the first world map (made by Anaximander, 550 BC), the world's oldest map (Konya town map, 6200 BC), the first map to use latitude and longitude lines (Ptolemy's world map), and the Vinland Map (first map of America). Students may create a poster or brochure to display their research.

Name _____

Map Skills Vocabulary Matchup

Directions: Cut apart the words and definitions. Make educated guesses to match each word with its definition. When you are positive that you have matched the words and definitions correctly, glue each word to one side of an index card. Glue its definition to the other side. Use the flash cards to study the vocabulary.

scale	**a representation of a region on a flat surface**
title	**a short description of a map's subject**
longitude lines	**a figure on a map used to display the orientation of north, south, east, and west**
map	**the explanation of the symbols on a map**
grid	**the size of an area on a map or globe compared with the actual size of the area on Earth**
compass rose	**a pattern of lines running horizontally and vertically that cross each other at right angles**
latitude lines	**the imaginary lines on a map or globe running east and west**
map legend or key	**the imaginary lines on a map or globe running north and south**

Name _____

Make a Map

Part 1

Directions: Work with a partner to create a map of the neighborhood where your school is located. Learn about the area by taking a walk around it with an adult. Study other maps of the area. Then, follow the checklist below as you create your map.

☐ Map title *(score ___/5 points)*

☐ Compass rose *(score ___/5 points)*

☐ Streets (at least 5) *(score ___/10 points)*

☐ Map legend or key *(score ___/20 points)*

☐ Symbols (at least 10) *(score ___/20 points)*

☐ Scale *(score ___/10 points)*

☐ Grid *(score ___/10 points)*

☐ Project neatness *(score ___/10 points)*

Part 2

Directions: On the back of your map, write directions from one place to another. Your route must use at least three streets. Use direction words, such as *north*, *south*, *east*, and *west*. Use street names and landmark descriptions to make your directions more clear.

☐ Written directions *(score ___/10 points)*

Total Points: _____ **/100 points**

Teacher Comments: _____

_____

_____

_____

_____

_____

_____

_____

_____

_____

Name _____

Make a Map

Part 1

Directions: Work with a partner to create a map of your school building. Start by taking a walk through the halls. Make notes about the relative sizes of rooms, the locations of stairways and restrooms, and the number of entrances. Then, follow the checklist below as you create your map.

☐ Map title *(score ___/5 points)*

☐ Compass rose *(score ___/5 points)*

☐ Classrooms and common areas *(score ___/10 points)*

☐ Entrances and stairways *(score ___/5 points)*

☐ Map legend or key *(score ___/20 points)*

☐ Symbols (at least 10) *(score ___/20 points)*

☐ Scale *(score ___/10 points)*

☐ Grid *(score ___/5 points)*

☐ Project neatness *(score ___/10 points)*

Part 2

Directions: On the back of your map, write directions from one place to another. Your route must use at least three hallways. Use direction words, such as *north*, *south*, *east*, and *west*.

☐ Written directions *(score ___/10 points)*

Total Points: _____ **/100 points**

Teacher Comments: _____

_____

_____

_____

_____

_____

_____

_____

_____

Name _____

Make a Map

Part 1

Directions: Work with a partner to create a map of your classroom. Start by taking a walk around the class. Make notes about the specific areas in your classroom. Then, follow the checklist below as you create your map.

☐ Map title *(score ___/5 points)*

☐ Compass rose *(score ___/5 points)*

☐ Classroom areas *(score ___/10 points)*

☐ Entrances *(score ___/10 points)*

☐ Map legend or key *(score ___/20 points)*

☐ Symbols (at least 10) *(score ___/20 points)*

☐ Scale *(score ___/10 points)*

☐ Grid *(score ___/10 points)*

☐ Project neatness *(score ___/10 points)*

Total Points: _____ **/100 points**

Teacher Comments: _____

_____

_____

_____

_____

_____

_____

_____

_____

_____

_____

_____

_____

American Indians and the Environment

Differentiation Strategy

 Tiered Graphic Organizers

Standards

- Students will understand the effects geography has had on the different aspects of societies.
- TESOL: Students will use nonverbal communication appropriate to audience, purpose, and setting.

Materials

- lesson resources (pages 138–141)
- clipboards
- books and websites about American Indians (See page 167.)
- photos of the environment in Florida, Alaska, Arizona, and Minnesota (optional)

Procedures

1 Ask students to imagine that the classroom is their environment. Within this environment, they must find everything they need to survive for many years. Ask the class to think about the needs that will arise over time. Make a list of ideas on the board. The list should include ideas such as *food, shelter, clothing, tools, traditions,* and *entertainment.*

2 Allow students to choose partners for a scavenger hunt. Give each pair a clipboard and lined paper. Instruct them to list *food, shelter, clothing, tools, traditions,* and *entertainment* as headings on their papers. Ask them to search the classroom for survival ideas that fit each category. Have them list these ideas on their papers. Challenge students to think creatively during this activity.

3 After about 10 minutes, bring the whole class back together. It is not necessary for students to fill their categories completely. The importance of this activity is getting students to think about having to depend on the environment for survival. Invite students to share their ideas.

4 Make the connection between the scavenger hunt activity and the lives of people hundreds of years ago. Explain that American Indians living long ago had to find ways to survive in their environments. They could not go to the grocery store to buy food. They could not call a realtor when they needed a new house. They did not go to the mall to buy clothes. The tribes had to make everything they needed from the environment around them.

5 Ask students to think about how the environment made life different for tribes in Florida and Alaska or for tribes in Arizona and Minnesota. Students may benefit from seeing photos of the places being compared during the class discussion. Explain that for the next activity, students will look for clues to answer the essential question: *How did the environment influence the lives of American Indians?*

American Indians and the Environment

6 Place students in six heterogeneous groups. Assign each group one of the following regions of the United States to research—the Northeast, the Southeast, the Great Lakes, the Plains, the Southwest, and the Northwest. Explain that the American Indian tribes in each of these regions had many things in common. Instead of studying one tribe, students should research all of the native people in their region and make generalizations about life there.

7 Show students the resources available for their research. Then, distribute the *American Indians and the Environment Research Notes* activity sheet (page 138) to students. Review the activity with the class and answer questions about the information students need to find.

8 Instruct each group to divide the research by topic and assign each member a specific topic to research. However, all students should read about their region's environment in order to answer the activity's essential question. Consider pairing below-grade-level students with on-grade-level students to conduct research.

★ **English Language Support**—Assign these students the important task of finding illustrations and photos to provide visual information.

9 After students have completed their research, they will compare their findings with students from another group. Distribute the *American Indians and the Environment* activity sheets (pages 139–141) to students based on their readiness levels.

10 Circulate and assist as students work. When students finish, regroup as a class and have them summarize their learning.

11 If students finish early, they may complete the Anchor Activity.

Assessment

Use the rubric below to assess students' understanding.

3	2	1
Graphic organizer is complete.	Graphic organizer is partially complete.	Graphic organizer is not complete at all.
Student fully answered the essential question.	Student answered the essential question.	Student did not answer the essential question.
Student's work shows a full understanding of the American Indians and their regions.	Student's work shows a partial understanding of the American Indians and their regions.	Student's work shows a lack of understanding of the American Indians and their regions.

Activity Levels
▲
Above Grade Level
■
On Grade Level
●
Below Grade Level

Anchor Activity

Have students read an American Indian legend from the region that they researched. As they read, students should ask themselves, *"Which details give information about the environment in which this story was created?"* Have students make a list of these details.

Name _____

American Indians and the Environment
Research Notes

Essential Question: *How did the environment influence the lives of American Indians?*

Directions: Research the American Indians of the _____ region.

Describe the land, climate, plants, animals, and other resources in the region.

_____

_____

_____

_____

_____

_____

_____

Use the table below to take notes about the American Indians you are researching.

Shelter	Food
Clothing	**Tools**
Traditions	**Entertainment**

Name _____

American Indians and the Environment

Part 1

Directions: Meet with the other students who have the same graphic organizer. There should be a student in your group representing each region. Compare your data.

Then, take what you have learned about tribes in your region and place them in two different regions. What adjustments would they have to make in these new locations? Then, fill in your graphic organizers below.

My Region _____

Environmental Factors	Necessary Adjustments
Region _____	
Region _____	

Part 2

Directions: Work with your group to answer the essential question—How did the environment influence the lives of American Indians?

_____
_____
_____
_____
_____
_____
_____
_____

Name _____

American Indians and the Environment

Part 1

Directions: Meet with two other students who have the same graphic organizer. Make sure they researched different regions. Compare your data. Then, complete the Venn diagram to examine the similarities and differences between the people of the three regions.

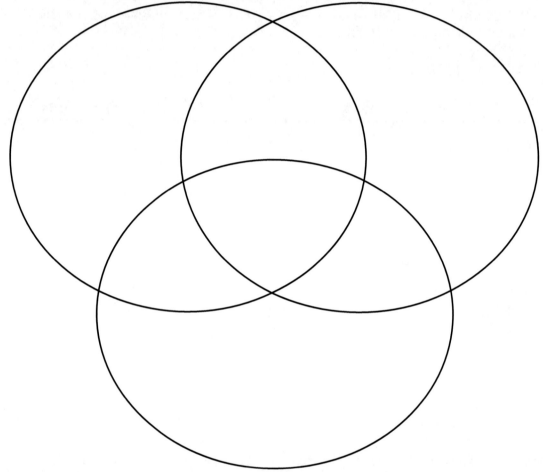

Part 2

Directions: Work with your partners to answer this essential question: *How did the environment influence the lives of American Indians?*

_____

_____

_____

_____

_____

_____

_____

_____

Name _____

American Indians and the Environment

Part 1

Directions: Meet with one other student who has the same graphic organizer. Make sure that person researched a different region. Compare your data. Then, complete the Venn diagram to compare and contrast the people of the two regions.

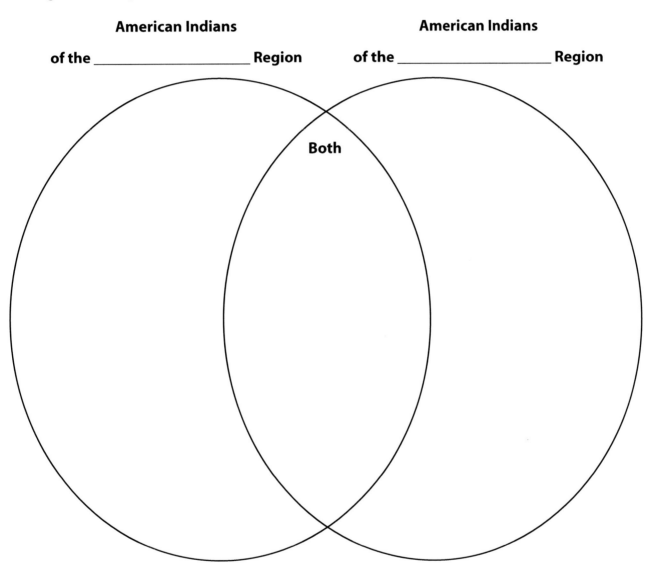

American Indians

of the _____ Region

American Indians

of the _____ Region

Both

Part 2

Directions: Describe three ways American Indians depended on the environment.

_____

_____

_____

_____

The Age of Exploration

Differentiation Strategy

 Choices Board

Standards

- Students will understand European explorers of the fifteenth and sixteenth centuries, their reasons for exploring, the information gained from their journeys, and what happened as a result of their travels.

- TESOL: Students will use appropriate learning strategies to construct and apply academic knowledge.

Materials

- lesson resources (pages 144–147)

- photo of Columbus (filename: columbus.jpg)

- audio recorder

- art supplies

- blank world maps

- books and websites about the Age of Exploration (*See page 167.*)

Procedures

Preparation Note: Write the following seven reasons for exploration on sheets of paper: curiosity, wealth, fame, national pride, religion, foreign goods, and better trade routes. Tape these words to the board.

❶ Ask students to guess the category that connects all of the words on the board. (The correct answer is *reasons for exploration*.) Explain that these seven things motivated the explorers of the fifteenth and sixteenth centuries to venture into the unknown and face terrible dangers. Their journeys changed our world in many ways.

❷ Explain each reason in more detail to give students a better understanding of European explorers' motives for exploration.

> *Curiosity*—People wondered who and what was out there in the world.
>
> *Wealth*—People wanted to find things that would make them rich.
>
> *Fame*—People wanted to make a name for themselves with their discoveries.
>
> *National pride*—People explored to claim territory for their countries.
>
> *Religion*—People traveled to tell others about the Christian religion.
>
> *Foreign goods*—People wanted to bring back spices and jewels.
>
> *Better trade routes*—People wanted to find faster ways to get to Asia.

❸ Place students in seven heterogeneous groups. Assign each group one of the seven reasons for exploration. Instruct students to keep their topics secret.

❹ Display the photo of the Christopher Columbus statue in New York City's Central Park found on the Teacher Resource CD. Ask students to study the statue and describe what this work of art says about the famous explorer.

The Age of Exploration

5 Explain to students that each group will create a living statue that portrays its assigned reason for exploration. Essentially, the students will imagine a scene that portrays the reason for exploration. They will make simple costumes and props and pose in the scene to look like a statue. Every member of the group must be part of the statue, even if they are posing as an inanimate object or an animal. Allow time for groups to prepare their statues. (Time will vary depending on the level of detail desired from the living statues.)

6 After students have created their living statues, invite groups to the front of the classroom, one by one. Have them strike the pose and hold it for about 30 seconds as the audience studies the work of art. Give the audience three tries to guess the reason for the exploration being portrayed. Ask each group to verify the correct answer and to explain how its scene can help students remember that reason for exploration.

7 Tell students that they will have a chance to find out more about specific explorers and how their discoveries changed the world. These activities will involve independent research and are best used as an extended homework assignment.

8 Distribute the *Exploring the Past Choices Board* activity sheet (page 144) to students. They will each complete one activity at their readiness level independently and one challenging activity with a friend. Above-grade-level students should complete two above-level activities. Another option is to distribute the *Exploring the Past Choices Cards* activity sheets (pages 145–147) to students based on readiness levels. This will allow them to choose activities at their levels only.

★ **English Language Support**—Read the choices aloud to English language learners. Make necessary adjustments for written work by having students record their answers or present them to you orally.

9 If students finish early, they may complete the Anchor Activity.

Assessment

Assess students as they work on their projects. Do this by meeting with students in small groups to answer questions along the way and also by checking to make sure that students are following directions and giving their best work.

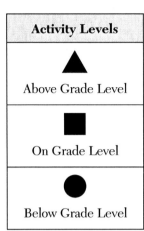

Activity Levels
▲
Above Grade Level
■
On Grade Level
●
Below Grade Level

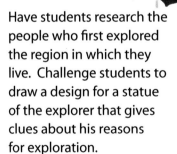

Anchor Activity

Have students research the people who first explored the region in which they live. Challenge students to draw a design for a statue of the explorer that gives clues about his reasons for exploration.

Name _____

Exploring the Past Choices Board

Directions: Choose two activities from the choices board. Be sure to match the shape(s) assigned to you by your teacher.

I will choose a _____ activity to complete by myself and a _____ activity to complete
with a friend. (shape)   (shape)

Make a set of explorer trading cards. On each card, include an illustration of the explorer and his full name on the front. On the back of the card, include fun facts about his life and discoveries. ■	Choose an explorer you want to learn more about. Research the explorer's life and discoveries. Then, write a skit about one of the explorer's discoveries. △	Choose one explorer you want to learn more about. Research the explorer's life and discoveries. Then, make a time line showing the important dates and events in his life. ○
Mark the routes of at least three different explorers on a world map. Use different colors to mark each route. Use special symbols to show important places on the map. Add a map key that explains the colors and symbols. ○	Choose one explorer you want to learn more about. Write and illustrate a picture book that tells the story of the explorer's exciting life in a way younger kids would enjoy. ■	Modern-day explorers use technology that early explorers did not have. Research the tools modern-day sailors and explorers use. Compare and contrast these tools with the tools early explorers used. Create a comparison chart to show the similarities and differences. △
Design a card game or a board game about the Age of Exploration. Let the games you like to play inspire your ideas. Create the game and teach your classmates how to play. △	Design a series of four explorer postage stamps to commemorate the Age of Exploration. On four large pieces of paper, create your stamp designs. Make sure each stamp gives clues about the person's life and discoveries. ○	Choose one explorer you want to learn more about. Imagine that you are the explorer. Write a postcard to your family back home. On the front of the postcard, draw a landscape that shows a sight you have seen. On the other side of the postcard, write a short letter telling about the trip. ■

Name _____

Exploring the Past Choices Cards

Directions: Choose activities from the cards below.

Choose an explorer you want to learn more about. Research the explorer's life and discoveries. Then, write a skit about one of the explorer's discoveries.	Modern-day explorers use technology that early explorers did not have. Research the tools modern-day sailors and explorers use. Compare and contrast these tools with the tools early explorers used. Create a comparison chart to show the similarities and differences.
Design a card game or a board game about the Age of Explorations. Let the games you like to play inspire your ideas. Create the game and teach your classmates how to play.	Free choice—Think of your own question to research. Make a product that will show what you found out. Get the teacher's approval before beginning.

Name _____

Exploring the Past Choices Cards

Directions: Choose activities from the cards below.

Make a set of explorer trading cards. On each card, include an illustration of the explorer and his full name on the front. On the back of the card, include fun facts about his life and discoveries.

Choose one explorer you want to learn more about. Write and illustrate a picture book that tells the story of the explorer's exciting life in a way younger kids would enjoy.

Choose one explorer you want to learn more about. Imagine that you are the explorer. Write a postcard to your family back home. On the front of the postcard, draw a landscape that shows a sight you might have seen. On the other side of the postcard, write a short letter telling about your trip.

Free choice—Think of your own question to research. Make a product that will show what you found out. Get the teacher's approval before beginning.

© *Shell Education*

Name _____

Exploring the Past Choices Cards

Directions: Choose activities from the cards below.

Choose one explorer you want to learn more about. Research the explorer's life and discoveries. Then, make a time line showing the important dates and events in his life.	Mark the routes of at least three different explorers on a world map. Use different colors to mark each route. Use special symbols to show important places on the map. Add a map key that explains the colors and symbols.
Design a series of four explorer postage stamps to commemorate the Age of Exploration. On four large pieces of paper, create your stamp designs. Make sure each stamp gives clues about the person's life and discoveries.	Free choice—Think of your own question to research. Make a product that will show what you found out. Get the teacher's approval before beginning.

History's Heroes

Differentiation Strategy

Multiple Intelligences

Standards

- Students will understand how the ideas of significant people affected the history of the state.

- TESOL: Students will use appropriate learning strategies to construct and apply academic knowledge.

Materials

- lesson resources (pages 150–153)

- photos of wax statues (See page 167.)

- list of famous people in your state (country) history

- books and websites about state history (See page 167.)

- art supplies

Procedures

Note: This is a multi-day lesson.

❶ Engage students with photos of realistic wax statues of famous people. Then, tell students that they will work together to make a "wax" museum of their own.

❷ Post a list of famous people in your state's (or country's) history. Students will research these important people to learn about their contributions to history. Group the students heterogeneously. Assign each group one or more people from the list. Show students the resources available for their research.

★ **English Language Support**—If possible, provide resources for students at their independent reading levels. Another option is to pair these students with reading buddies or classroom volunteers who can read the texts aloud and point out key facts.

❸ Distribute copies of the *History's Heroes Research Guide* activity sheet (page 150) to students. Read the directions and questions aloud to the whole class. Circulate and assist as students complete their research.

❹ When all groups have finished the research guides, the work on the wax museum will begin. Distribute *History's Heroes Wax Museum Jobs List* activity sheet (page 151) to students. Review the activities with the class and have students put stars next to the activities that interest them the most.

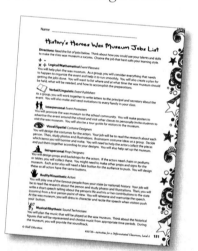

History's Heroes

5 Students who chose the same activities should meet as a group. Distribute copies of the *History's Heroes Project Planner* activity sheet (page 152). Have students begin brainstorming ideas and making a list of the steps that they will take. Meet with each group to review the directions and provide guidance. Set a clear time line for students to complete project milestones.

6 On the day of the wax museum, students will use their special abilities to make the event a success. The students who choose kinesthetic activities will dress up and portray the historical figures. The students who choose interpersonal activities will be tour guides for visitors. The students who choose visual/spatial activities will set up the event and assist the actors with costumes and props.

7 Students may complete the Anchor Activity as an extension.

Assessment

Use the *History's Heroes Project Rubric* (page 153) to assess student projects.

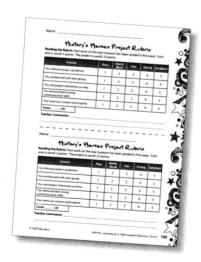

Anchor Activity

Have students learn basic facts about each person on the list of famous people in history. Then, have students rank the people in order of their importance. The rankings are opinions, but students must justify their choices in writing next to each person's name on the list.

Name _____

History's Heroes Research Guide

Directions: Read about the life of the person you were assigned. Then, answer the questions below to keep track of the important facts about the person's life.

What was the person's full name? _____

Where was the person born? _____

Where did the person live? _____

Why is this person important to the state's (country's) history?

_____

_____

_____

_____

_____

_____

What other interesting facts should we know about this person?

_____

_____

_____

_____

_____

_____

Sketch and color a picture of the person in the space below or on the back of this page. Be sure to add details such as the person's clothing and accessories.

Name _____

History's Heroes Wax Museum Jobs List

Directions: Read the list of jobs below. Think about how you could use your talents and skills to make the class wax museum a success. Choose the job that best suits your learning style.

 Logical/Mathematical *Event Planners*

You will help plan the wax museum. As a group, you will consider everything that needs to happen to organize the event and help it to run smoothly. You will also create a plan for getting the jobs done. You will want to list where and at what time the wax museum should be held, what will be needed, and how to accomplish the preparations.

 Verbal/Linguistic *Event Publishers*

As a group, you will work together to write letters to the principal and secretary about the event. You will also make and send invitations to every family in your class.

 Interpersonal *Event Promoters*

You will promote the wax museum to the school community. You will make posters to advertise the event around the school and visit other classes to personally invite students to visit the wax museum. You will also be a tour guide for visitors to the museum.

 Visual/Spatial *Costume Designers*

You will design the costumes for the actors. Your job will be to read the research about each person. Then, study photos and illustrations. Brainstorm costume ideas as a group. Decide which items you will borrow and make. You will need to help the actors collect the pieces and put them together according to your designs. You will also help set up the museum.

 Intrapersonal *Prop Designers*

You will design props and backdrops for the actors. If the actors need chairs or podiums or tables, you will collect these. You might need to make other props and signs for the museum. Each actor also will need a fake button for the audience to push. You will design these so all actors have the same buttons.

 Bodily/Kinesthetic *Actors*

You will play one of the famous people from your state (or national) history. Your job will be to read the research about the person and study photos and illustrations. Then, you will write a short speech telling about the person's life and his or her contributions to the state (country) from a first-person point of view. You will rehearse and memorize the speech. At the wax museum, you will dress in character and recite the speech when visitors push your button.

Musical/Rhythmic *Sound Technicians*

You will plan the music that will be played at the wax museum. Think about the historical figures that will be represented and choose music from appropriate time periods. During the museum, you will provide the soundtrack.

Name _____

History's Heroes Project Planner

Directions: Read the example given on the chart. Then, complete the chart below to help plan your project.

My job for the wax museum is _____

Action Steps	Important Information	Results	Next Meeting Date
• go to library to research clothes • find photos • photocopy photos	*Meet teacher at copy machine on Tuesday during lunch*	*All copies made*	*Friday during class*

© Shell Education

Name _____

History's Heroes Project Rubric

Reading the Rubric: Your work on the wax museum has been graded in five areas. Each area is worth 5 points. The project is worth 25 points.

Criteria	Poor	Needs Work	Fair	Strong	Excellent
You followed project guidelines.	1	2	3	4	5
You worked well with your group.	1	2	3	4	5
You met project milestones on time.	1	2	3	4	5
You demonstrated strong communication skills.	1	2	3	4	5
Your work was creative and original.	1	2	3	4	5

Score: _____ / 25

Teacher Comments: _____

_____

- -

Name _____

History's Heroes Project Rubric

Reading the Rubric: Your work on the wax museum has been graded in five areas. Each area is worth 5 points. The project is worth 25 points.

Criteria	Poor	Needs Work	Fair	Strong	Excellent
You followed project guidelines.	1	2	3	4	5
You worked well with your group.	1	2	3	4	5
You met project milestones on time.	1	2	3	4	5
You demonstrated strong communication skills.	1	2	3	4	5
Your work was creative and original.	1	2	3	4	5

Score: _____ / 25

Teacher Comments: _____

_____

Supply and Demand

Differentiation Strategy

 Menu of Options

Standards

- Students will understand that businesses are willing and able to sell more of a product when its price goes up and less when its price goes down.

- TESOL: Students will use English to interact in the classroom.

Materials

- lesson resources (pages 156–159)
- candy or small prizes
- index cards
- art supplies
- books and websites about supply and demand *(See page 167.)*

Procedures

1 Introduce students to basic economic principles with a simple economic simulation. Place a jar of candy or small prizes at the front of the classroom. At this point, there should be only a few pieces in the jar. Tell students that this is the *supply*—the amount of goods or services available for purchase. Since you provided the candy or prizes, that makes you the *producer*—the person or business that provides goods and services.

2 Build on the simulation by asking students if they want the candy or prizes. Ask them how much they are willing to pay for the goods. Explain that their desire for the goods is the *demand*. Buying the goods would make them *consumers*—the buyers of a good or service. Ask them to think about the price students would be willing to pay for the items in the jar if you brought it to the cafeteria during lunch. Explain that high prices are due to *scarcity*—not enough supply to satisfy the demand.

3 Add more items to the jar. This time, there should be plenty of candy or prizes for everyone in the class. Ask students to think about what they would pay for the candy (prizes) now. Explain that the price goes down when there is more supply than demand. Tell them that they have just learned the *law of supply and demand*—the theory that an increase in supply will lower prices and an increase in demand will raise prices.

4 As you explain each component of the scenario, define the related vocabulary term. Then, label the item with the word written on an index card. For example, place the label *supply* on the jar of candy.

★ **English Language Support**—English language learners will benefit from taking part in this vocabulary activity. Seeing examples and acting out the scenario will place the words in context and help students to remember them.

Supply and Demand

5 Expand the discussion to goods and services with which students are familiar. For example, discuss the latest holiday gift craze that had parents lining up early in the morning outside stores and paying high prices online. Discuss what will happen to the price of that item next year when it is replaced by a new popular item.

6 Distribute the *Supply and Demand Menu of Options* (pages 156–157). Explain to students that they will choose activities from the menu to learn more about economic principles. They may also choose to propose alternative or additional projects for your approval. Decide ahead of time how many points students need to complete from the menu. Have students use the *Supply and Demand Project Planning Guide* activity sheet (page 158) to prepare for their projects.

7 If students finish early, they may complete the Anchor Activity.

Assessment

Use the *Supply and Demand Rubric* (page 159) to assess students' work. You may want to create a general criteria chart with the students to clarify how they will be evaluated. Criteria may include creativity, completeness, and neatness.

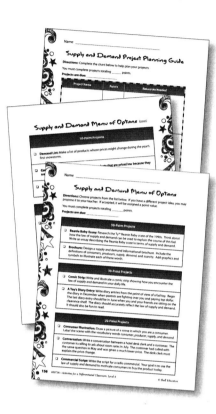

Anchor Activity

Have students make up a game based on the law of supply and demand. The game should involve buying and selling goods or services, and might be similar to *Monopoly*®.

Name _____

Supply and Demand Menu of Options

Directions: Choose projects from the list below. If you have a different project idea, you may propose it to your teacher. If accepted, it will be assigned a point value.

You must complete projects totaling _____ points.

Projects are due: _____

50-Point Projects

❑ **Beanie Baby Essay:** Research the Ty™ Beanie Baby craze of the 1990s. Think about how the law of supply and demand can be used to explain the course of this fad. Write an essay describing the Beanie Baby craze in terms of supply and demand.

❑ **Brochure:** Design a supply and demand informational brochure. Include the definitions of *consumers*, *producers*, *supply*, *demand*, and *scarcity*. Add graphics and symbols to illustrate each of these words.

30-Point Projects

❑ **Comic Strip:** Write and illustrate a comic strip showing how you encounter the law of supply and demand in your daily life.

❑ **A Toy's Diary Entry:** Write diary entries from the point of view of a fad toy. Begin the diary in December when parents are fighting over you and paying top dollar. The last diary entry should be in June when you and your friends are sitting on the clearance shelf. The diary should accurately reflect the law of supply and demand. It should also be fun to read.

20-Point Projects

❑ **Consumer Illustration:** Draw a picture of a scene in which you are a consumer. Label the scene with the vocabulary words *consumer*, *producer*, *supply*, and *demand*.

❑ **Conversation:** Write a conversation between a hotel desk clerk and a customer. The customer is calling to ask about room rates in July. The customer had called with the same question in May and was given a much lower price. The desk clerk must explain the price change.

❑ **Commercial Script:** Write the script for a radio commercial. Your goal is to use the law of supply and demand to motivate consumers to buy the product today.

© *Shell Education*

Supply and Demand Menu of Options *(cont.)*

10-Point Projects

❑ **Demand List:** Make a list of products whose prices might change during the year's first snowstorm.

❑ **Common Goods List:** Make a list of five products that are priced low because they are common and easy to get.

❑ **Scarce Goods List:** Make a list of five products that are priced high because they are rare and hard to get.

Student-Proposed Projects

❑ _____

_____

_____

_____

❑ _____

_____

_____

_____

_____

Name _____

Supply and Demand Project Planning Guide

Directions: Complete the chart below to help plan your projects.

You must complete projects totaling _____ points.

Projects are due: _____

Project Name	Points	Resources Needed
Total Points:	**Notes:**	

Name _____

Supply and Demand Rubric

Directions: Use the chart below to evaluate student work.

Project Comments	Points Possible	Points Earned

Total Points: _____

Teacher Comments: _____

_____

— —

Name _____

Supply and Demand Rubric

Directions: Use the chart below to evaluate student work.

Project Comments	Points Possible	Points Earned

Total Points: _____

Teacher Comments: _____

State Government

Differentiation Strategy

 Leveled Questions

Standards

- Students will understand the major responsibilities of the legislative, executive, and judicial branches of their state government.

- TESOL: Students will use appropriate learning strategies to construct and apply academic knowledge.

Materials

- lesson resources (pages 162–165)

- chart paper and markers

- books and websites about students' state government *(See page 167.)*

- overhead or LCD projector

- 2 flyswatters

Procedures

❶ Have students participate in a "popcorn" sharing activity. In this activity, students will randomly "pop up" from their seats, share something they know about state government or government in general, and sit back down. Record students' ideas on the board or on chart paper. Conclude the activity by explaining the basic structure and function of their state government.

❷ Divide the class into two heterogeneous teams. Explain that the teams will be competing in a state-government scavenger hunt. Each team member will be responsible for finding certain facts about their state-government. Students may use textbooks, the Internet, and additional resources to research the state government.

❸ Assign students a shape based on their readiness levels. Distribute the level-appropriate portion of the *State Government Scavenger Hunt* activity sheet (page 162) to students.

★ **English Language Support**—Read the questions aloud to these students. Help them highlight key words and phrases. Model for them how to scan text for those key words and phrases.

❹ After students complete the scavenger hunt, bring the class back together for a review game. Have them sit with their scavenger-hunt teammates. The game is called *Swat*.

❺ In the game, *Swat*, you will project a copy of the *State Government Swat Game Board* activity sheet (page 163) onto a wall. Be sure to fill in your current state senator, judge, and governor.

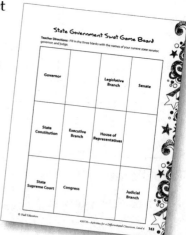

State Government

6 Choose one player from each team to stand on either side of the projected activity sheet. Make sure the players who compete against each other are in the same readiness groups. For example, call two students from the square group at the same time. Hand each player a flyswatter.

7 Use the *State Government Swat Questions and Answers* (pages 164–165) to ask questions for the game. Make sure that the questions asked were part of the students' scavenger hunt. Read the question aloud. The players will compete to be first to swat the correct answer on the wall. The student who swats the correct answer on the wall first gets one point for his or her team. If players get stuck on a question, they should raise their hands. This is a signal for their teammates to provide assistance.

Activity Levels
▲
Above Grade Level
■
On Grade Level
●
Below Grade Level

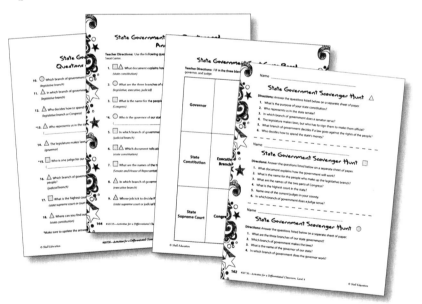

8 If students finish early, they may complete the Anchor Activity.

Assessment

Observe students as they work in teams and ask questions of them to assess their understanding. Document students' level of participation while working in groups and playing the game.

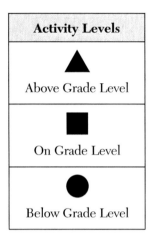

Anchor Activity

Have students help teammates complete the scavenger hunt and then read through all the questions to prepare for the *Swat* game.

Name _____

State Government Scavenger Hunt ▲

Directions: Answer the questions listed below on a separate sheet of paper.

1. What is the purpose of your state constitution?
2. Who represents us in the state senate?
3. In which branch of government does a senator serve?
4. The legislature makes laws, but who has to sign them to make them official?
5. What branch of government decides if a law goes against the rights of the people?
6. Who decides how to spend the state's money?

– –

Name _____

State Government Scavenger Hunt ◻

Directions: Answer the questions listed below on a separate sheet of paper.

1. What document explains how the government will work?
2. What is the name for the people who make up the legislative branch?
3. What are the names of the two parts of Congress?
4. What is the highest court in the state?
5. Name one of the current judges in your county.
6. In which branch of government does a judge serve?

– –

Name _____

State Government Scavenger Hunt ●

Directions: Answer the questions listed below on a separate sheet of paper.

1. What are the three branches of our state government?
2. Which branch of government makes the laws?
3. What is the name of the governor of our state?
4. In which branch of government does the governor work?

State Government Swat Game Board

Teacher Directions: Fill in the three blanks with the names of your current state senator, governor, and judge.

Governor		Legislative Branch	Senate
State Constitution	Executive Branch	House of Representatives	
State Supreme Court	Congress		Judicial Branch

State Government Swat Questions and Answers

Teacher Directions: Use the following questions and answers for the State Government Swat Game.

1. ☐△ What document explains how the government will work?

    (state constitution)

2. ◯ What are the three branches of our state government?

    (legislative, executive, judicial)

3. ☐ What is the name for the people who make up the legislative branch?

    (Congress)

*4. ◯ Who is the governor of our state?

    (_____)

5. ☐ In which branch of government does a judge serve?

    (judicial branch)

6. ☐△ Which document tells about the three branches of government?

    (state constitution)

7. ☐ What are the names of the two parts of Congress?

    (Senate and House of Representatives)

8. △ In which branch of government does the governor work?

    (executive branch)

9. △ Whose job is it to decide if laws go against people's rights?

    (state supreme court or judicial branch)

© *Shell Education*

State Government Swat
Questions and Answers *(cont.)*

10. ◯ Which branch of government makes the laws?

(legislative branch)

11. △ In which branch of government does a senator serve?

(legislative branch)

12. △ Who decides how to spend the state's money?

(legislative branch or Congress)

*13. △ Who represents us in the state senate?

(_____)

14. △ The legislature makes laws, but who has to sign them to make them official?

(governor)

*15. ☐ Who is one judge for our county?

(_____)

16. △ Which branch of government decides if a law goes against the rights of the people?

(judicial branch)

17. ☐ What is the highest court in the state?

(state supreme court or court of appeals)

18. △ Where can you find out how the branches of state government work together?

(state constitution)

*Make sure to update the answers to questions 4, 13, and 15 regularly.

References

Bess, J. 1997. *Teaching well and liking it: Motivating faculty to teach effectively.* Baltimore, MD: The Johns Hopkins University Press.

Brandt, R. 1998. *Powerful learning.* Alexandria, VA: Association for Supervision and Curriculum Development.

Bruner, J. 2004. *Toward a theory of instruction.* Cambridge, MA: Belnap Press of Harvard University Press.

Costa, A. L., and R. Marzano. 1987. Teaching the language of thinking. *Educational Leadership* 45: 29–33.

Gardner, H. 1983. *Frames of mind: The theory of multiple intelligences.* New York: Basic Books.

———. 1999. *Intelligence reframed: Multiple intelligences for the 21st Century.* New York: Basic Books.

Jensen, E. 1998. *Teaching with the brain in mind.* Alexandria, VA: Association for Supervision and Curriculum Development.

Olsen, K. D. 1995. *Science continuum of concepts: For grades K–6.* Black Diamond, WA: Books for Educators.

Sprenger, M. 1999. *Learning and memory: The brain in action.* Alexandria, VA: Association for Supervision and Curriculum Development.

Teele, S. 1994. Redesigning the educational system to enable all students to succeed. PhD diss., University of California, Riverside.

Winebrenner, S. 1992. *Teaching gifted kids in the regular classroom.* Minneapolis, MN: Free Spirit Publishing.

Additional Resources

Where books and websites are referenced in lesson materials lists, some suggestions for these resources are provided below. Shell Education does not control the content of these websites, or guarantee their ongoing availability, or links contained therein. We encourage teachers to preview these websites before directing students to use them.

Page 28—Writing Dialogue

Cleary, Beverly. *Ralph S. Mouse*. New York: HarperTrophy, 2006.

Kehoe, Tim. *The Unusual Mind of Vincent Shadow*. Boston: Little Brown Books for Young Readers, 2009.

McDonald, Megan. *Judy Moody*. Cambridge, MA: Candlewick Press, 2000.

Osborne, Mary Pope. *Dinosaurs Before Dark*, Magic Tree House. New York: Random House, 1992.

Trueit, Trudi. *No Girls Allowed (Dogs Okay)*, Secrets of a Lab Rat. New York: Aladdin, 2010.

Page 34—Summarizing

Child, Lauren. *The Princess and the Pea*. New York: Hyperion Book, 2006.

Sendak, Maurice. *Where the Wild Things Are*. New York: HarperCollins, 1988.

Van Allsburg, Chris. *Jumanji*. Boston: Houghton Mifflin, 1981.

White, Linda. *Too Many Pumpkins*. White Plains, NY: Live Oak Media, 2004.

Page 46—Story Elements

Eisen, Armand. *A Treasury of Children's Literature*. Boston: Houghton Mifflin, 1992.

Posnot, Marie. *The Golden Book of Fairy Tales*. New York: Golden Books Publishing, 1999.

Page 52—Haiku Poetry

Gollub, Matthew. *Cool Melons—Turn to Frogs!: The Life and Poems of Issa*. New York: Lee & Low Books, 2004.

Mannis, Celeste. *One Leaf Rides the Wind*. New York: Puffin, 2005.

www.famouspoetsandpoems.com

www.poets.org

Page 94—The Water Cycle and Weather

Breen, Mark and Kathleen Friestad. *The Kid's Book of Weather Forecasting*. Nashville, TN: Ideals, 2008.

Cosgrove, Brian. *Weather*. New York: DK Children, 2007.

http://ga.water.usgs.gov (search water cycle)

www.weatherchannelkids.com_

Page 100—The Moon

Trammel, Howard K. *The Solar System*. Danbury, CT: Children's Press, 2010.

www.kidsastronomy.com (search moon)

Page 112—Life Cycles

Crewe, Sabrina. *The Salmon*. Boston: Steck-Vaughn, 1998.

Kalman, Bobbie and Kathryn Smithyman. *The Life Cycle of a Frog*. New York: Crabtree Publishing, 1997.

Trumbauer, Lisa. *The Life Cycle of a Grasshopper*. Mankato, MN: Pebble Books, 2003.

www.sciencenewsforkids.org

Page 118—How Animals Adapt

www.audobon.org

Page 124—Erosion

Bailey, Jacqui. *Cracking Up: A Story about Erosion*. Mankato, MN: Picture Window Books, 2006.

www.nature.nps.gov (search erosion)

Page 136—American Indians and the Environment

Murdoch, David S. *North American Indian*. New York: DK Children, 2005.

www.history.com

Page 142—Age of Exploration

Elliott, Lynne. *Exploration in the Renaissance*. New York: Crabtree Publishing, 2009.

Flowers, Sarah. *The Age of Exploration*. Farmington Hills, MI: Greenhaven Press, 1999.

Page 148—History's Heroes

Celebrate the States, 2nd ed., series. New York: Benchmark Books, 2005–2010.

Miller, Millie, and Cyndi Nelson. *The United States of America: A State-by-State Guide*. New York: Scholastic, 1999.

www.madametussauds.com

Page 154—Supply and Demand

Loewen, Nancy. *Lemons and Lemonade: A Book about Supply and Demand*. Mankato, MN: Picture Window Books, 2005.

Thompson, Gare. *What is Supply and Demand?* New York: Crabtree Publishing, 2009.

Page 160—State Government

Silberdick, Barbara Feinberg. *State Governments*. London: Franklin Watts, 1993.

www.kids.gov (search states)

Contents of the Teacher Resource CD

Lesson Resource Pages

Page	Lesson	Filename
24–27	Self-Editing	pg024.pdf
30–33	Writing Dialogue	pg030.pdf
36–39	Summarizing	pg036.pdf
42–45	Main Idea and Supporting Details	pg042.pdf
48–51	Story Elements	pg048.pdf
54–57	Haiku Poetry	pg054.pdf
60–63	Number Sense	pg060.pdf
66–69	Decimals	pg066.pdf
72–75	Measuring and Graphing	pg072.pdf
78–81	Fractions	pg078.pdf
84–87	Perimeter and Area	pg084.pdf
90–93	Geometric Transformations	pg090.pdf
96–99	The Water Cycle and Weather	pg096.pdf
102–105	The Moon	pg102.pdf
108–111	States of Matter	pg108.pdf
114–117	Life Cycles	pg114.pdf
120–123	How Animals Adapt	pg120.pdf
126–129	Erosion	pg126.pdf
132–135	Map Skills	pg132.pdf
138–141	American Indians and the Environment	pg138.pdf
144–147	The Age of Exploration	pg144.pdf
150–153	History's Heroes	pg150.pdf
156–159	Supply and Demand	pg156.pdf
162–165	State Government	pg162.pdf

Image Resources

Page	Image	Filename
126	Antelope Canyon	antelope.jpg
126	Arbol de Piedra	arbol.jpg
127	Half Dome	dome.jpg
127	Hidden Lake	lake.jpg
127	Happisburgh	happisburgh.jpg
127	Cathedral Cove Beach	cove.jpg
142	Christopher Columbus	columbus.jpg

Teacher Resources

Title	Filename
Answer Key	answers.pdf
Bingo Board	bingo.pdf
Cause-and-Effect Graphic Organizer	causeeffect.pdf
Comic Strip	comic.pdf
T-Chart	tchart.pdf
Three Column Chart	threecolumn.pdf
Time Line	timeline.pdf
Triple Venn Diagram	triplevenn.pdf
Venn Diagram	venn.pdf